SELECTED PRAYERS

مختارات من الدعاء

A Collection Of Du'a' From The Qur'an and Sunnah

Compiled by
Jamal A. Badawi

Published by
Ta-Ha Publishers
1, Wynne Road,
London SW9 0BD, United Kingdom

Arkān - ᶜIbādāt Series No. 6

6th Edition 1413/1993

Published by
Ta-Ha PUBLISHERS Ltd.
1 Wynne Road
LONDON SW9 0BB
Tel: 071-737 7266/7
Fax: 071-737 7267

British Library Cataloguing in Publication Data

Badawi, Jamal A.
Selected Prayers: Collection of Dua from
the Qur'an and Sunnah — 6 Rev. ed
I. Title
297

ISBN 0-907461-90-5

Library of Congress Catalog Card No. 79-54076

Printed By: DELUXE PRINTERS Tel: 081-965 1771

TABLE OF CONTENTS

بسم الله الرحمن الرحيم

ولسوف يعطيك ربك فترضى

PREFACE

بِسْمِ ٱللَّهِ ٱلرَّحْمَٰنِ ٱلرَّحِيمِ

My gratitude is due to Allāh Subḥānahu Wat^{c}āla for being able to make this booklet on du^{c}ā’ available to our English-speaking brothers and sisters. The booklet contains both the transliteration and the translation of each du^{c}ā’. It is hoped that this dual feature will help in reciting them and in understanding what is being recited.

I pray to Allāh that He bless those who use these du^{c}ā’ in inculcating a relationship of nearness to Him and in responding to His eternal loving call.

When My servants
Ask thee concerning Me,
I am indeed
Close (to them): I listen
To the prayer of every
Suppliant when he calleth on Me:
Let them also, with a will,
Listen to My call,
And believe in Me:
That they may walk
In the right way.

وَإِذَا سَأَلَكَ عِبَادِى عَنِّى فَإِنِّى قَرِيبٌ ۖ
أُجِيبُ دَعْوَةَ ٱلدَّاعِ إِذَا دَعَانِ ۖ فَلْيَسْتَجِيبُوا۟
لِى وَلْيُؤْمِنُوا۟ بِى لَعَلَّهُمْ يَرْشُدُونَ ﴿١٨٦﴾

(Al-Qur’ān, 2:186)

Why Was the Book Compiled

The idea to compile a book of du^{c}ā’ developed in the summer of 1977 in the course of my participation in the Imam Training Programs. It was then that several brothers and sisters expressed the wish that the du^{c}ā’ which they were learning orally might well be published in a booklet to be made available to all who wished to recite, and benefit from them.

How was it Compiled

1. The first chapter was compiled following a review of the Qur'ān and taking note of the Āyāt or its portions which constitute du^{c}ā'. These were then studied and classified under their main subject headings.

2. The remaining du^{c}ā' in Chapters 2, 3, and 4 were selected and compiled from Hasan Al-Bânnā's <u>Al-Mathoorāt</u>, an excellent collection of du^{c}ā'. The order of some du^{c}ā' in Chapters 3 and 4 differ slightly from that in Al-Ma'thoorāt.

3. All transliteration was done by the author according to the system indicated in the book. The translations of the Qur'ānic du^{c}ā' were taken from A. Yusuf Ali's The Glorious Qur'ān. The other du^{c}ā' in Chapters 2, 3 and 4 were translated by the author.

4. A word about the footnotes. Each note indicates the source of the du^{c}ā' and in some cases gives a brief comment on it. The number of each note refers to the serial number of the du^{c}ā' in the text.

5. Br. Anwer Beg, Editor of Publications in the ITC has been very helpful in editing this work and in other related matters.

To Sister Sherene El-Fayoumy goes the credit of accurate and difficult typing especially in the transliterations.

Jamal A. Badawi

8 Laurel Lane, Halifax, N.S.

Canada B3M 2P6

Phone: (902)445-2494

Introduction*

Meaning of Thikr:

Thikr literally means remembrance. As used in this booklet, it refers to the remembrance of Allah (S.W.T.)** The Qur'ān refers to itself as thikr.*** As the word of Allāh (S.W.T.), it helps us remember Him in all our thoughts and deeds.

Thikr at all times:

Each human being pursues an ultimate and fundamental goal in life. This goal constitutes one's ideal, the focal point of one's thoughts, aspirations, and activities. The loftier and nobler this goal is, the more sublime are the thoughts and deeds emanating from it.

The basic message of Islam is to elevate the soul, to purify and uplift it to the highest possible plain. This cannot be accomplished unless Allāh (S.W.T.) is our Ultimate Goal and the focus of our life.

There is no wonder then that the Prophet (S.A.W.)**** used to engage in thikr at all times.

---

* This introduction is based on Hasan Albannā's *Al-Ma'Thoorāt*, Maktabat-ul-Manār, Kuwait, n.d., pp. 5—12.

** (S.W.T.) = Subhānaho Wata[c]ālá = Glory be to Him, Most High.

*** See Al-Qur'ān, 15:9

**** (S.A.W.) — Sâllâl-lāho [c]Alâyhî Wâsâllâm = May Allāh's peace and blessings be upon him.

Following the Prophet's example, thikr should be part of our daily life. Thikr is not only limited to words; it includes also meditation, reflection, repentance, seeking lawful provisions and, generally, every lawful act during which the presence of Allāh (S.W.T.) is felt.

Rewards for Thikr:

Among the numerous passages in the Qur'ān which deal with thikr are the following:

O ye who believe!
Celebrate the praises of Allah,
And do this often;

يَٰٓأَيُّهَا ٱلَّذِينَ ءَامَنُوا۟ ٱذْكُرُوا۟ ٱللَّهَ ذِكْرًا كَثِيرًا ﴿٤١﴾

And glorify Him
Morning and evening.

وَسَبِّحُوهُ بُكْرَةً وَأَصِيلًا ﴿٤٢﴾

He it is Who sends
Blessings on you, as do
His angels, that He may
Bring you out from the depths
Of Darkness into Light:
And He is Full of Mercy
To the Believers.

هُوَ ٱلَّذِى يُصَلِّى عَلَيْكُمْ وَمَلَٰٓئِكَتُهُۥ لِيُخْرِجَكُم
مِّنَ ٱلظُّلُمَٰتِ إِلَى ٱلنُّورِ ۚ وَكَانَ بِٱلْمُؤْمِنِينَ
رَحِيمًا ﴿٤٣﴾

(Al-Qur'ān, 33:41-43)

For Muslim men and women, —
For believing men and women,
For devout men and women,
For true men and women,
For men and women who are
Patient and constant, for men
And women who humble themselves,
For men and women who give
In charity, for men and women
Who fast (and deny themselves),
For men and women who
Guard their chastity, and
For men and women who

إِنَّ ٱلْمُسْلِمِينَ وَٱلْمُسْلِمَٰتِ وَٱلْمُؤْمِنِينَ
وَٱلْمُؤْمِنَٰتِ وَٱلْقَٰنِتِينَ وَٱلْقَٰنِتَٰتِ وَٱلصَّٰدِقِينَ
وَٱلصَّٰدِقَٰتِ وَٱلصَّٰبِرِينَ وَٱلصَّٰبِرَٰتِ وَٱلْخَٰشِعِينَ
وَٱلْخَٰشِعَٰتِ وَٱلْمُتَصَدِّقِينَ وَٱلْمُتَصَدِّقَٰتِ
وَٱلصَّٰٓئِمِينَ وَٱلصَّٰٓئِمَٰتِ وَٱلْحَٰفِظِينَ
فُرُوجَهُمْ وَٱلْحَٰفِظَٰتِ وَٱلذَّٰكِرِينَ
ٱللَّهَ كَثِيرًا وَٱلذَّٰكِرَٰتِ أَعَدَّ ٱللَّهُ لَهُم
مَّغْفِرَةً وَأَجْرًا عَظِيمًا ﴿٣٥﴾

Engage much in Allah's praise,—
For them has Allah prepared
Forgiveness and great reward,

(Al-Qur'ān, 33:35)

In a Qudsi hadeeth, the Prophet (S.A.W.) reported that Allāh (S.W.T.) said: "I (will respond according to) what my servant thinks of Me, and I am with him when he remembers Me. So if he remembers Me in secret, I will remember him in secret and if he remembers Me in a group, I will remember him in a better group." (Al-Bukhāri, Muslim)

Manners in Thikr:

To bear fruit, the following points should be observed in thikr:

i) Humility, sobriety and reflection on the meaning of du‘ā’.

ii) Lowering one's voice and avoiding disruption of others engaged in thikr.

And do thou (O reader!)
Bring thy Lord to remembrance
In thy (very) soul,
With humility and in reverence,
Without loudness in words,
In the mornings and evenings;
And be not thou
Of those who are unheedful.

وَٱذۡكُر رَّبَّكَ فِي نَفۡسِكَ تَضَرُّعٗا وَخِيفَةٗ
وَدُونَ ٱلۡجَهۡرِ مِنَ ٱلۡقَوۡلِ بِٱلۡغُدُوِّ وَٱلۡأٓصَالِ
وَلَا تَكُن مِّنَ ٱلۡغَٰفِلِينَ ٢٠٥

(Al-Qur'ān, 7:205)

(iii) Cleanliness and respectability of clothes and of the place of thikr.

By observing these rules, the person will feel happiness in heart, light in soul and blessings of Allāh (S.W.T.).

Thikr in a Group:

Engaging in thikr is permissible in groups. Indeed, it is encouraged in some aḥādeeth.

The following is an example:

The Prophet (S.A.W.) said: “If a group of people sit together remembering Allāh (i.e. engaging in thikr), the angels will circle them, the mercy will shroud them, the peace will descend onto them and Allāh will remember them among those with Him.” (Muslim)

Indeed thikr in a group may help teach those who do not know the desired duʿā’ and bring Muslims’ hearts together and strengthen their noble ties.

Transliteration System

In transliterating Arabic words, the following system of symbols has been used.

I. Arabic Consonants with English Equivalents

Arabic	English	Example	Arabic	English	Example
ب	b	book	ش	sh	shield
ت	t	toy	ف	f	fast
ث	ṫh	three	ك	k	key
ج	j	joy	ل	l	light
د	d	door	م	m	mother
ذ	th	this	ن	n	number
ر	r	ran	هـ	h	humble
ز	z	zeal	و	w,ao	Laos
س	s	sand	ى	y	yard

II. Arabic Consonants with no English Equivalents

Arabic	English	Example	Arabic	English	Example
ء	’	Qur’ān	ط	ṭ	Ṭaharah
ح	ḥ	Ḥasan	ظ	ẓ	Ẓuhr
خ	kh	Khomaini	ع	c	cAbdullah
ص	ṣ	Ṣahih	غ	gh	Ghayb
ض	ḍ	Wuḍu	ق	q	Qur’ān

III. Elongation: A Macron indicates long vowels:

ā = long a as (aa) in band and Qur'ān

ī = long i as (ee) in peel and Ḥadīth (Ḥadeeth)

ū = long u as (oo) in tooth and Qunūt.

IV. Assimilation of the definite article (al) in Arabic:

When the above article (al) precedes a dental, sibilant n, t, r, the (l) is assimilated in pronounciation of the following letter. Therefore, in transliteration the word is written as it is pronounced and not as it is actually written in Arabic. Example:

An-Nasā'ī (not Al-Nasā'ī)

At-Tirmithi (not Al-Tirmithī)

Ash-Shāfi'ī (not Al-Shāfi'ī)

V. Shortening of Sounds in Words

When this symbol [ˆ] is used above a letter the sound is very much shortened as the [a] in woman, German or American.

Chapter One

Duᶜā’ From The Qur’ān

I. On Īmān (Faith)

A. Confirmation of Īmān

(1)

Say: "Verily, I am commanded
To serve Allah
With sincere devotion;

قُلْ إِنِّىٓ أُمِرْتُ أَنْ أَعْبُدَ ٱللَّهَ مُخْلِصًا لَّهُ ٱلدِّينَ ﴿١١﴾

"And I am commanded
To be the first
Of those who bow
To Allah in Islam."
(39:11-12)

وَأُمِرْتُ لِأَنْ أَكُونَ أَوَّلَ ٱلْمُسْلِمِينَ ﴿١٢﴾

Qul Innī Omêrtô-ân A^{c}bodâllahâ Mukhlisâl-lâhoddīn. Wâ'omêrto-li'ân Akoonà-awwâlâl-muslimeen

(2)

"Our Lord! we believe
In what Thou hast revealed,
And we follow the Apostle;
Then write us down
Among those who bear witness."
(3:53)

رَبَّنَآ ءَامَنَّا بِمَآ أَنزَلْتَ وَٱتَّبَعْنَا ٱلرَّسُولَ
فَٱكْتُبْنَا مَعَ ٱلشَّٰهِدِينَ ﴿٥٣﴾

Râbbânā Aamannā-bîmā-anzâltâ-wâttâbâ^c nârrâsoolâ-fâktobnā Mâ^{c}âsh-shāhideen

(3)

"Our Lord is
The Lord of the heavens
And of the earth: never
Shall we call upon any god
Other than Him: if we
Did, we should indeed
Have uttered an enormity!
(18:14)

رَبُّنَا رَبُّ
ٱلسَّمَٰوَٰتِ وَٱلْأَرْضِ لَن نَّدْعُوَا۟ مِن دُونِهِۦٓ إِلَٰهًا
لَّقَدْ قُلْنَآ إِذًا شَطَطًا ﴿١٤﴾

Râbbonā Râbbos-sâmāwati Wâl'arḍi-lân-nâd^{c}ôwâ-min-doonihī-ilāha. Lâqâd-qulnā-ithân-shaṭatā

(4)

'We have faith,
And do thou bear witness
That we bow to Allah
As Muslims'."

(5:111)

ءَامَنَّا وَٱشْهَدْ بِأَنَّنَا مُسْلِمُونَ ﴿١١١﴾

Aamânnā Wâsh-hâd Bi'ânnā Muslimoon

(5)

Say: Will ye dispute
With us about Allah, seeing
that He is our Lord
And your Lord; that we
Are responsible for our doings
And ye for yours; and that
We are sincere (in our faith)
In him?

(2:139)

قُلْ أَتُحَآجُّونَنَا فِي ٱللَّهِ وَهُوَ رَبُّنَا وَرَبُّكُمْ وَلَنَآ
أَعْمَٰلُنَا وَلَكُمْ أَعْمَٰلُكُمْ وَنَحْنُ لَهُۥ مُخْلِصُونَ ﴿١٣٩﴾

Qul Atoḥājjūnânā Fil-lāhî Wâhowâ Râbbonā wârâbbokum wâlânā
A^{c}mālona Wâlâkum A^{c}mālukum Wânâhnô Lâhoo Mukhlisoon

(6)

Say thou: "This is my Way:
I do invite unto Allah,—
On evidence clear as
The seeing with one's eyes,—

I and whoever follows me.
Glory to Allah! and never
Will I join gods with Allah!"

(12:108)

قُلْ هَٰذِهِۦ سَبِيلِىٓ أَدْعُوٓا۟ إِلَى ٱللَّهِ ۚ عَلَىٰ بَصِيرَةٍ
أَنَا۠ وَمَنِ ٱتَّبَعَنِى ۖ وَسُبْحَٰنَ ٱللَّهِ
وَمَآ أَنَا۠ مِنَ ٱلْمُشْرِكِينَ ﴿١٠٨﴾

Qul Hāthihi sâbeelī-ad^{c}oo-Ilâl-lāhi-^{c}âlā Basīrâtin Anâ-Wâmânit-tâbâ^{c}âni Wâsubhānâl-lahi Wâmā Anâ-minâl-Mushrikeen.

B. Glorification of Allah

(7)

Glory to the Lord
Of the heavens and the earth,
The Lord of the Throne
(Of Authority)! (He is
Free) from the things
They attribute (to Him)!
(43:82)

سُبۡحَٰنَ رَبِّ ٱلسَّمَٰوَٰتِ وَٱلۡأَرۡضِ رَبِّ ٱلۡعَرۡشِ
عَمَّا يَصِفُونَ ٨٢

Subḥānâ-Râbbis-Sâmāwatî-Wâl'arḍî-Râbbil-^{c}Arshî-^{c}Ammā Yaṣifoon

(8)

Glory to Allah!
(High is He)
Above the partners
They attribute to Him.
(59:23)

سُبۡحَٰنَ ٱللَّهِ عَمَّا يُشۡرِكُونَ ٢٣

Subḥānâl-Lāhi-^{c}Ammā Yushrikoon

(9)

Blessed be the name
Of thy Lord,
Full of Majesty,
Bounty and Honour.
(55:78)

تَبَٰرَكَ ٱسۡمُ رَبِّكَ ذِى ٱلۡجَلَٰلِ وَٱلۡإِكۡرَامِ ٧٨

Tâbārâkâsmo-râbbikâ thil-Jâlālî Wâl-ikrām

(10)

Praise and glory be
To Him! (for He is) above
What they attribute to Him!
To Him is due
The primal origin
Of the heavens and the earth:
How can He have a son
When He hath no consort?
He created all things,
And He hath full knowledge
Of all things.
(6:100-101)

سُبۡحَٰنَهُۥ وَتَعَٰلَىٰ عَمَّا يَصِفُونَ ١٠٠

بَدِيعُ ٱلسَّمَٰوَٰتِ وَٱلۡأَرۡضِۖ أَنَّىٰ يَكُونُ لَهُۥ وَلَدٞ
وَلَمۡ تَكُن لَّهُۥ صَٰحِبَةٞۖ وَخَلَقَ كُلَّ شَيۡءٖۖ
وَهُوَ بِكُلِّ شَيۡءٍ عَلِيمٞ ١٠١

Subhānâho Wât^{c}ālā ^{c}Ammā Yâṣifoon Bâdī^{c}os Sâmāwati Wâl'arḍ . Annā Yâkoono Lâho Wâlâdon-Wâlâm Tâkun Lâhō Ṣāhibatuw-wâkhâlâqâ-kullâ Shây'. Wâhowâ-Bikullî-Shây'in-^{c}Âleem

(11)

For Allah is One God:
Glory be to Him:
(Far Exalted is He) above
Having a son. To Him
Belong all things in the heavens
And on earth. And enough
Is Allah as a Disposer of affairs.
(4:171)

إِنَّمَا ٱللَّهُ إِلَٰهٌ وَٰحِدٌ سُبْحَٰنَهُۥٓ أَن
يَكُونَ لَهُۥ وَلَدٌ لَّهُۥ مَا فِى ٱلسَّمَٰوَٰتِ
وَمَا فِى ٱلْأَرْضِ وَكَفَىٰ بِٱللَّهِ وَكِيلًا ﴿١٧١﴾

Innâmâl-lâho Ilāhow-wāhid. Subhānâho Ay-yâkoonâ Lâho Wâlad. Lâho Mā-Fis-Sâmāwatî-Wâmā-Fil-arḍ Wâkâfā Billāhi-Wâkeelā

(12)

So blessed be Allah,
The Best to create!
(23:14)

فَتَبَارَكَ ٱللَّهُ أَحْسَنُ ٱلْخَٰلِقِينَ ﴿١٤﴾

Fâtâbārâkâl-lâho Aḥsânol-khāliqeen

(13)

And blessed is He
To Whom belongs the dominion
Of the heavens and the earth,
And all between them:
With Him is the knowledge
Of the Hour (of Judgment):
And to Him shall ye
Be brought back.
(43.85)

وَتَبَارَكَ ٱلَّذِى لَهُۥ مُلْكُ ٱلسَّمَٰوَٰتِ وَٱلْأَرْضِ وَمَا بَيْنَهُمَا
وَعِندَهُۥ عِلْمُ ٱلسَّاعَةِ وَإِلَيْهِ تُرْجَعُونَ ﴿٨٥﴾

Wâtâbārâkâl-lâthi Lāhoo Mulkus-Sâmāwati-Wâl'arḍî-Wâmā-Bâynahomā-Wâ^{c}indâho-^{c}Ilmus-sā^{c}âtî Wâ'ilayhî-Turjâ^{c}oon

(14)

Blessed is He Who made
Constellations in the skies,
And placed therein a Lamp
And a Moon giving light;
(25:61)

تَبَارَكَ ٱلَّذِى جَعَلَ فِى ٱلسَّمَآءِ بُرُوجًا وَجَعَلَ فِيهَا
سِرَٰجًا وَقَمَرًا مُّنِيرًا ﴿٦١﴾

Tâbārâkâl-lâthi-Jâ^{c}âlâ-Fis-sâmā'î Buroojaw-wâjâ^{c}âlâ Fîhā-Sirājâw-wâqâmârâm-muneerā

(15)

And to govern? Blessed
Be Allah, the Cherisher
And Sustainer of the Worlds!
(7:54)

أَلَا لَهُ ٱلْخَلْقُ
وَٱلْأَمْرُ ۗ تَبَارَكَ ٱللَّهُ رَبُّ ٱلْعَٰلَمِينَ ﴿٥٤﴾

Alā Lâhol-khâlqo-Wâl'amr Tâbārâkâl-lāho Râbbol-^{c}ālâmîn

(16)

So celebrate with praises
The name of thy Lord
The Supreme.
(56:96)

فَسَبِّحْ بِٱسْمِ رَبِّكَ ٱلْعَظِيمِ ﴿٩٦﴾

Fâsâbbiḥ-Bismî-Râbbikâl-^{c}âẓeem

(17)

But celebrate the praises
Of thy Lord, and be of those
Who prostrate themselves
In adoration.
(15:98)

فَسَبِّحْ بِحَمْدِ رَبِّكَ وَكُن مِّنَ ٱلسَّٰجِدِينَ ﴿٩٨﴾

Fâsâbbiḥ Biḥâmdî Râbbikâ Wâkom-Minâs-sājideen

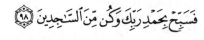

(18)

"And they say: 'Glory
To our Lord! Truly
Has the promise of our Lord
Been fulfilled!'"
(17:108)

سُبْحَٰنَ رَبِّنَآ إِن كَانَ وَعْدُ رَبِّنَا لَمَفْعُولًا ﴿١٠٨﴾

Subḥānâ Râbbinā In Kânâ Wâ^{c}dô Râbbinā Lâmâf^{c}oolā

(19)

So (give) glory to Allah,
When ye reach eventide
And when ye rise
In the morning;
(30:17)

فَسُبْحَٰنَ ٱللَّهِ حِينَ تُمْسُونَ وَحِينَ تُصْبِحُونَ ﴿١٧﴾

Fâsobḥānâl-lāhî Ḥeenâ Tumsoonâ Wâḥeenâ Tuṣbiḥoon

(20)

"Our Lord! not for naught
Hast Thou created (all) this!
Glory to Thee! Give us
Salvation from the Penalty
Of the Fire.
(3:191)

رَبَّنَا مَا خَلَقْتَ هَٰذَا بَٰطِلًا سُبْحَٰنَكَ
فَقِنَا عَذَابَ ٱلنَّارِ ﴿١٩١﴾

Râbbâna Mā-Khâlâqtâ Hāthā Bāṭilân Subḥānakâ-Fäqina ^{c}Athāban-nār

(21)

So glory to Him
In Whose hands is
The dominion of all things:
And to Him will ye
Be all brought back.
(36:83)

فَسُبْحَٰنَ ٱلَّذِى بِيَدِهِۦ مَلَكُوتُ كُلِّ شَىْءٍ
وَإِلَيْهِ تُرْجَعُونَ ﴿٨٣﴾

Fâsobhānâl-lâthī-Bîyâdihi Mâlâkootô-Kullî-Shây'iw Wâilâyhî Turjâ^{c}oon

(22)

Blessed be He
In Whose hands
Is Dominion;
And He over all things
Hath Power;—
(67:1)

تَبَٰرَكَ ٱلَّذِى بِيَدِهِ ٱلْمُلْكُ وَهُوَ عَلَىٰ كُلِّ شَىْءٍ قَدِيرٌ ﴿١﴾

Tâbārâkâl-lâthi-Biyâdîhîl-mulkû Wâhowâ ^{c}Alā Kullî-shây'in Qâdeer

(23)

Such is Allah your Lord.
So Glory to Allah,
The Lord of the Worlds!
(40:64)

ذَٰلِكُمُ ٱللَّهُ رَبُّكُمْ ۖ فَتَبَارَكَ ٱللَّهُ رَبُّ
ٱلْعَٰلَمِينَ ﴿٦٤﴾

Thālikumul-lāho Râbbukum Fâtâbārâkâ-llāhô Râbbôl-^{c}Ālâmeen

(24)

Glorify the name
Of thy Guardian-Lord
Most High,
(87:1)

سَبِّحِ ٱسْمَ رَبِّكَ ٱلْأَعْلَى ﴿١﴾

Sâbbiḥ-îsmâ Râbbikâl-A^{c}lā

(25)

Celebrate the Praises
Of thy Lord, and pray
For His Forgiveness:
For He is Oft-Returning
(In Grace and Mercy).
(110:3)

فَسَبِّحْ بِحَمْدِ رَبِّكَ وَٱسْتَغْفِرْهُ ۚ إِنَّهُۥ
كَانَ تَوَّابًۢا ﴿٣﴾

Fâsâbbiḥ Biḥâmdî-Râbbikâ-Wâstâghfirh. Innâhō kānâ Tâwwābā

(26)

Whatever is
In the heavens and
On earth, doth declare
The Praises and Glory
Of Allah: to Him belongs
Dominion, and to Him belongs
Praise: and He has power
Over all things.
(64:1)

يُسَبِّحُ لِلَّهِ مَا فِي ٱلسَّمَٰوَٰتِ وَمَا فِي ٱلْأَرْضِ لَهُ ٱلْمُلْكُ
وَلَهُ ٱلْحَمْدُ وَهُوَ عَلَىٰ كُلِّ شَيْءٍ قَدِيرٌ ١

Yosâbbiḥo-Lillāhî-Māfis-sâmāwatî-Wâmā Fil-arḍ. Lâhol-Mulkû-Wâlâhol-ḥamd. Wâhowâ-cAlā-kullî-shây'in Qâdeer.

C. Submission to, and Dependence on, Allāh

(27)

To Allah do belong
The unseen (secrets)
Of the heavens and the earth,
And to Him goeth back
Every affair (for decision):
Then worship Him,
And put thy trust in Him:
And thy Lord is not
Unmindful of aught
That ye do.
(11:123)

وَلِلَّهِ غَيْبُ ٱلسَّمَٰوَٰتِ وَٱلْأَرْضِ وَإِلَيْهِ يُرْجَعُ
ٱلْأَمْرُ كُلُّهُۥ فَٱعْبُدْهُ وَتَوَكَّلْ عَلَيْهِ
وَمَا رَبُّكَ بِغَٰفِلٍ عَمَّا تَعْمَلُونَ ١٢٣

Wâlillāhi Ghâybos-Sâmāwatî-Wâl'arḍ. Wa'ilâyhî Yurjâcol-amrô-Kulloh. Fâcbodhô-Wâtâwâkkâl-cAlâyh Wâmā-Râbbokâ-Bighāfilin-cAmmā Tâcmâloon

(28)

"I put my trust in Allah
My Lord and your Lord!
There is not a moving
Creature, but He hath
Grasp of its fore-lock.
Verily, it is my Lord
That is on a straight Path.
(11:56)

إِنِّي تَوَكَّلْتُ عَلَى ٱللَّهِ رَبِّي وَرَبِّكُم مَّا مِن دَآبَّةٍ إِلَّا هُوَ
ءَاخِذٌۢ بِنَاصِيَتِهَآ إِنَّ رَبِّي عَلَىٰ صِرَٰطٍ مُّسْتَقِيمٍ ٥٦

Inni Tâwâkkâltô-cAlâl-lāhi-Râbbi-Wârâbbî-Kum Mā-Min-Dâbbâtin Illā Hôwâ-Ākhithom-Bînāṣiyâtihā Innâ-Râbbî-cAlā Ṣirātim-Mustâqeem

(29)

"I have submitted
My whole self to Allah
And so have those
Who follow me."
(3:20)

أَسْلَمْتُ وَجْهِىَ لِلَّهِ وَمَنِ ٱتَّبَعَنِ

Aslâmtô Wâjhiyâ Lillāhî Wâmânit-tâbâ^{c}ân

(30)

Say: "He is (Allah)
Most Gracious: we have
Believed in Him,
And on Him have we
Put our trust:
So, soon will ye know
Which (of us) it is
That is in manifest error."
(67:29)

قُلْ هُوَ ٱلرَّحْمَٰنُ ءَامَنَّا بِهِۦ وَعَلَيْهِ تَوَكَّلْنَا فَسَتَعْلَمُونَ
مَنْ هُوَ فِى ضَلَٰلٍ مُّبِينٍ ﴿٢٩﴾

Qul Howâr-râḥmānô-Āmânnā-Bihī-Wâ^{c}âlyhî tâwâkkâlnā. Fâstâ^{c}lâmoonâ-Mân-Howâ-Fi-Ḍālālim-mubeen

(31)

"For my Protector is Allah
Who revealed the Book
(From time to time),
And He will choose
And befriend the righteous.
(7.196)

إِنَّ وَلِـِّۧىَ ٱللَّهُ ٱلَّذِى نَزَّلَ ٱلْكِتَٰبَ وَهُوَ يَتَوَلَّى
ٱلصَّٰلِحِينَ ﴿١٩٦﴾

Innâ Wâllîyyiyâl-lāhôl-lâthī-Nâzzâlâl-kitābâ Wâhowâ-Yâtâwâllâṣ-Ṣalihin

(32)

"For me, I have set
My face, firmly and truly,
Towards Him Who created
The heavens and the earth,
And never shall I give
Partners to Allah"
(6:79)

إِنِّى وَجَّهْتُ وَجْهِىَ لِلَّذِى فَطَرَ ٱلسَّمَٰوَٰتِ
وَٱلْأَرْضَ حَنِيفًا وَمَآ أَنَا۠ مِنَ
ٱلْمُشْرِكِينَ ﴿٧٩﴾

Innī-Wâjjâhtô-Wâjhiyâ-lillâthi-Fâṭârâs-sâmāwātî-Wâl-arḍâ-Ḥâneefaw-wamā-Anâ Minâl-mushrikeen

(33)

Say: "Truly, my prayer
And my service of sacrifice,
My life and my death,
Are (all) for Allah,
The Cherisher of the Worlds:

قُلْ إِنَّ صَلَاتِي وَنُسُكِي وَمَحْيَايَ وَمَمَاتِي لِلَّهِ
رَبِّ الْعَالَمِينَ ﴿١٦٢﴾

No partner hath He:
This am I commanded,
And I am the first
Of those who bow
To His Will.
(6:162-163)

لَا شَرِيكَ لَهُ وَبِذَٰلِكَ أُمِرْتُ وَأَنَا أَوَّلُ الْمُسْلِمِينَ ﴿١٦٣﴾

Qul Innâ-Sâlāti Wânusuki Wâmâḥyāyâ-Wâmâmāti Lîllāhî-Râbbîl-^{c}Alâmeen Lā-Shâreekâ-Lâh Wâbithālikâ Omertô-Wâ'ânâ-Awwâlôl-muslimeen

(34)

"O our Lord! truly Thou
Dost know what we conceal
And what we reveal:
For nothing whatever is hidden
From Allah, whether on earth
Or in heaven.
(14:38)

رَبَّنَا إِنَّكَ تَعْلَمُ مَا نُخْفِي وَمَا نُعْلِنُ وَمَا يَخْفَىٰ عَلَى اللَّهِ
مِن شَيْءٍ فِي الْأَرْضِ وَلَا فِي السَّمَاءِ ﴿٣٨﴾

Râbbâna-Innâkâ-Ta^{c}lâmo-Mā-Nokhfi-Wâma-No^{c}lin Wâmā-Yâkhfā-^{c}Alâl-Lahi-Min-Shây'in-Fil-arḍi-Wâlā-Fis-sâmā'

(35)

Say: "O Allah!
Creator of the heavens
And the earth!
Knower of all that is
Hidden and open:
It is Thou that wilt
Judge between Thy Servants
In those matters about which
They have differed."
(39:46)

قُلِ اللَّهُمَّ فَاطِرَ السَّمَاوَاتِ وَالْأَرْضِ عَالِمَ الْغَيْبِ
وَالشَّهَادَةِ أَنتَ تَحْكُمُ بَيْنَ عِبَادِكَ
فِي مَا كَانُوا فِيهِ يَخْتَلِفُونَ ﴿٤٦﴾

Qulil-lahommâ-Fāṭirâs-sâmāwati Wâl'arḍ. ^{c}Alimâl-ghâybî-wâsh-shâhadâh. Antâ-Tâḥkumu Bâynâ-^{c}Ibādikâ-Fîma-Kānoo-Fihî-yâkhtâlifoon

(36)

"Who created me, and
It is He who guides me;

ٱلَّذِى خَلَقَنِى فَهُوَ يَهْدِينِ ﴿٧٨﴾

"Who gives me food and drink,

وَٱلَّذِى هُوَ يُطْعِمُنِى وَيَسْقِينِ ﴿٧٩﴾

"And when I am ill,
It is He who cures me;

وَإِذَا مَرِضْتُ فَهُوَ يَشْفِينِ ﴿٨٠﴾

"Who will cause me to die,
And then to live (again);

وَٱلَّذِى يُمِيتُنِى ثُمَّ يُحْيِينِ ﴿٨١﴾

"And who, I hope,
Will forgive me my faults
On the Day of Judgment.

وَٱلَّذِىٓ أَطْمَعُ أَن يَغْفِرَ لِى خَطِيٓـَٔتِى يَوْمَ ٱلدِّينِ ﴿٨٢﴾

(26:78:82)

Allâthī-Khâlâqâni-Fâhowâ-Yâhdeen. Wallathī Howâ-Yut^{c}imonī-Wâyâsqeen. Wa'ithā-Mâriḍtô-Fâhowâ-Yâshfeen. Wâllâthī-Yumeetonī-Thummâ-Yôhyeen. Wâllâthi-Aṭmâ^{c}ô-Ay-Yâghfīra-Lī-Khâṭee'âtī-Yâwmâd-dīn

(37)

And put thy trust
In Him Who lives
And dies not; and celebrate
His praise; and enough is He
To be acquainted with
The faults of His servants;—

وَتَوَكَّلْ عَلَى ٱلْحَىِّ ٱلَّذِى لَا يَمُوتُ وَسَبِّحْ
بِحَمْدِهِۦ ۚ وَكَفَىٰ بِهِۦ بِذُنُوبِ عِبَادِهِۦ خَبِيرًا ﴿٥٨﴾

(25:58)

Wâtâwâkkâl-^{c}Alâl-Ḥâyyil-Lâthi-Lā Yâmootô Wâsâbbiḥ-Bihâmdîh. Wâkâfā-Bihī-Bithonoobî-^{c}Ibādihī-Khâbeerā

II. Supplication

A. Seeking Guidance

(38)

"Unless my Lord
Guide me, I shall surely
Be among those
Who go astray."
(6:77)

لَئِن لَّمْ يَهْدِنِي رَبِّي لَأَكُونَنَّ مِنَ الْقَوْمِ
الضَّالِّينَ ﴿٧٧﴾

La'illâm Yâhdîni-Râbbi Lâ'akoonânnâ-Minâl-qâwmiḍ-ḍāl-leen

(39)

"I do hope
That my Lord will show me
The smooth and straight Path."
(28:22)

عَسَىٰ رَبِّي أَن يَهْدِيَنِي سَوَاءَ السَّبِيلِ ﴿٢٢﴾

^{c}Asā Râbbī Ay-yâhdiyânī Sâwā'âs-sâbeel'

(40)

"Our Lord! bestow on us
Mercy from Thyself,
And dispose of our affair
For us in the right way!"
(18:10)

رَبَّنَا آتِنَا مِن لَّدُنكَ رَحْمَةً وَهَيِّئْ لَنَا مِنْ أَمْرِنَا رَشَدًا ﴿١٠﴾

Râbbâna Ātîna Mil-lâdonkâ Râḥmâtâw-Wâhayyi' Lânā Min Amrinā Râshâdā

(41)

"Our Lord!" (they say),
"Let not our hearts deviate
Now after Thou hast guided us,
But grant us mercy
From Thine own Presence;
For Thou art the Grantor
Of bounties without measure.
(3:8)

رَبَّنَا لَا تُزِغْ قُلُوبَنَا بَعْدَ إِذْ هَدَيْتَنَا وَهَبْ لَنَا مِن لَّدُنكَ
رَحْمَةً إِنَّكَ أَنتَ الْوَهَّابُ ﴿٨﴾

Râbbânā Lā Tuzigh Quloobânā Bâ^{c}dâ Ith-hâdâytânā Wâhâb Lânā Mil-Lâdonkâ Râḥmâh. Innâkâ Antâl-Wâhhāb

B. Seeking Forgiveness (Istighfār)

(42)

"There is
No god but Thou:
Glory to Thee: I was
Indeed wrong!"
(21:87)

لَآ إِلَٰهَ إِلَّآ أَنتَ
سُبْحَٰنَكَ إِنِّى كُنتُ مِنَ ٱلظَّٰلِمِينَ ﴿٨٧﴾

Lā-Ilahâ-Illā Antâ Subḥānâkâ-Innī Kontô-Minaẓ-ẓālimeen

(43)

"O my Lord!
I have indeed wronged my soul!
(28:16)

رَبِّ إِنِّى ظَلَمْتُ نَفْسِى فَٱغْفِرْ لِى

Râbbî-innī Ẓâlâmtô-Nâfsī-Faghfirlī

(44)

"Our Lord! we have indeed
Believed: forgive us, then,
Our sins, and save us
From the agony of the Fire;"—
(3:16)

رَبَّنَآ إِنَّنَآ ءَامَنَّا فَٱغْفِرْ لَنَا
ذُنُوبَنَا وَقِنَا عَذَابَ ٱلنَّارِ ﴿١٦﴾

Râbbânā-Innânā-Āmânnā-Fâghfir-Lânā-Ẓonoobânā wâqina-ᶜathābân-Nār

(45)

"Glory
To our Lord! Verily we
Have been doing wrong!"
(68:29)

سُبْحَٰنَ رَبِّنَآ إِنَّا كُنَّا ظَٰلِمِينَ ﴿٢٩﴾

Subḥānâ-Râbbinā-Innā-Kunnā-Ẓālimeen

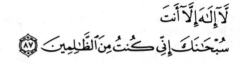

(46)

"Our Lord!
Condemn us not
If we forget or fall
Into error; our Lord!
Lay not on us a burden
Like that which Thou
Didst lay on those before us;

Our Lord! lay not on us
A burden greater than we
Have strength to bear.
Blot out our sins,
And grant us forgiveness.
Have mercy on us.
Thou art our Protector;
Help us against those
Who stand against Faith"
(2:286)

رَبَّنَا لَا تُؤَاخِذْنَآ إِن نَّسِينَآ
أَوْ أَخْطَأْنَا ۚ رَبَّنَا وَلَا تَحْمِلْ عَلَيْنَآ إِصْرًا
كَمَا حَمَلْتَهُۥ عَلَى ٱلَّذِينَ مِن قَبْلِنَا ۚ رَبَّنَا
وَلَا تُحَمِّلْنَا مَا لَا طَاقَةَ لَنَا بِهِۦ ۖ وَٱعْفُ عَنَّا
وَٱغْفِرْ لَنَا وَٱرْحَمْنَآ ۚ أَنتَ مَوْلَىٰنَا فَٱنصُرْنَا
عَلَى ٱلْقَوْمِ ٱلْكَٰفِرِينَ ﴿٢٨٦﴾

Râbbâna-Lā-Tu'ākhithnā-In-Nasīnā Ao Akhtâ'nā Râbbânā-Wâlā-Tâḥmil-^{c}Alâynā-Iṣrân-Kâma-Ḥâmâltâhō-^{c}Alâl-lâthīnâ-Min-qâblinā. Râbbânā-Wâlā-Toḥâmmilnā Malā-Ṭāqâtâ-Lânā Bêḥ. Wa^{c}fô-^{c}Annā-Wâghfir-Lânā-Wârḥâmnā Antâ mâolāna fânsornā ^{c}âlâl qâwmil-kāfireen

(47)

"Our Lord!
Forgive us, and our brethren
Who came before us
Into the Faith,
And leave not,
In our hearts,
Rancour (or sense of injury)
Against those who have believed.
Our Lord! Thou art
Indeed Full of Kindness,
Most Merciful."
(59:10)

رَبَّنَا ٱغْفِرْ لَنَا وَلِإِخْوَٰنِنَا ٱلَّذِينَ سَبَقُونَا
بِٱلْإِيمَٰنِ وَلَا تَجْعَلْ فِى قُلُوبِنَا غِلًّا لِّلَّذِينَ
ءَامَنُوا۟ رَبَّنَآ إِنَّكَ رَءُوفٌ رَّحِيمٌ ﴿١٠﴾

Râbbânâ-gh-fir-Lânā Wâl'ikhwāninâl-lâṭheenâ Sâbâqoonā Bil'īmān. Wâla-Tâj^{c}âl-Fi-Quloobinā-Ghillâl-lillâtheenâ-Āmânoo. Râbbânā-Innâkâ Râ'oofôr-Râḥeem

(48)

وَقُل رَّبِّ ٱغْفِرْ وَٱرْحَمْ وَأَنتَ خَيْرُ ٱلرَّٰحِمِينَ ﴿١١٨﴾

So say: "O my Lord!
Grant Thou forgiveness and mercy!
For Thou art the Best
Of those who show mercy!"
(23:118)

Wâqur-râbbi-gh-fir-Wârḥâm-Wâ'antâ-Khayrur-rāhimeen

(49)

سُبْحَٰنَكَ تُبْتُ إِلَيْكَ وَأَنَا۠ أَوَّلُ ٱلْمُؤْمِنِينَ ﴿١٤٣﴾

"Glory be to Thee! To Thee
I turn in repentance, and I
Am the first to believe."
(7:143)

Subḥānâkâ-Tubtû-Ilâykâ-Wâ'anā-Awwâl-ul-Mu'mineen

(50)

سَمِعْنَا وَأَطَعْنَا ۖ غُفْرَانَكَ رَبَّنَا
وَإِلَيْكَ ٱلْمَصِيرُ ﴿٢٨٥﴾

"We hear, and we obey:
(We seek) Thy forgiveness,
Our Lord, and to Thee
Is the end of all journeys."
(2:285)

Sami[c]-nā-Wa'aṭa[c]nā Ghufrānâkâ-Râbbânā Wâ'ilâykâl-Mâṣeer

C. Seeking Knowledge and Wisdom

(51)

وَقُل رَّبِّ زِدْنِى عِلْمًا ﴿١١٤﴾

"O my Lord! advance me
In knowledge."
(20:114)

Wâqur-râbbî-zidnī-[c]Ilmā

(52)

رَبِّ هَبْ لِى حُكْمًا
وَأَلْحِقْنِى بِٱلصَّٰلِحِينَ ﴿٨٣﴾

O my Lord! bestow wisdom
On me, and join me
With the righteous;
(26:83)

Râbbî-hâblī-Ḥukmâw-wâ'alḥiqni-Biṣṣāliheen

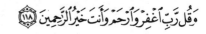

D. Prayer for Patience, Perseverance and Steadfastness

(53)

رَبَّنَا ٱكْشِفْ عَنَّا ٱلْعَذَابَ إِنَّا مُؤْمِنُونَ ﴿١٢﴾

"Our Lord! Remove
The Penalty from us,
For we do really believe!"
(44:12)

Râbbânâk-shif-[c]Annâl-[c]Athābâ-Innā-Mu'minoon

(54)

إِنَّمَآ أَشْكُوا۟ بَثِّى وَحُزْنِىٓ إِلَى ٱللَّهِ

"I only complain
Of my distraction and anguish
To Allah;
(12:86)

Innâmā-Ashkoo-Bâth-thi-Wâḥozni-Ilâl-lāh

(55)

رَبَّنَآ أَفْرِغْ عَلَيْنَا صَبْرًا وَثَبِّتْ أَقْدَامَنَا
وَٱنصُرْنَا عَلَى ٱلْقَوْمِ ٱلْكَٰفِرِينَ ﴿٢٥٠﴾

"Our Lord!
Pour out constancy on us
And make our steps firm:
Help us against those
That reject faith."
(2:250)

Râbbânā-Afrigh-[c]Alâynā-Sâbrâw-wâthâbbit-Aqdāmânā-Wânṣornā-[c]Alâl-qâwmil-kāfireen

(56)

رَبَّنَآ أَفْرِغْ عَلَيْنَا صَبْرًا وَتَوَفَّنَا مُسْلِمِينَ ﴿١٢٦﴾

Our Lord! pour out on us
Patience and constancy, and take
Our souls unto Thee
As Muslims (who bow
To Thy Will)!
(7:126)

Râbbânā-Afrigh-[c]Alâynā-Sâbrâw-wâtâwâffânā-Muslimeen

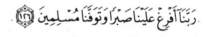

(57)

And do thou be patient,
For thy patience is but
From Allah; nor grieve over them:
And distress not thyself
Because of their plots.
For Allah is with those
Who restrain themselves,
And those who do good.
(16:127-128)

وَٱصۡبِرۡ وَمَا صَبۡرُكَ إِلَّا بِٱللَّهِۚ وَلَا تَحۡزَنۡ عَلَيۡهِمۡ
وَلَا تَكُ فِي ضَيۡقٖ مِّمَّا يَمۡكُرُونَ ١٢٧
إِنَّ ٱللَّهَ مَعَ ٱلَّذِينَ ٱتَّقَواْ وَّٱلَّذِينَ هُم
مُّحۡسِنُونَ ١٢٨

Wâṣbir-Wâmā-Ṣâbrokâ-Illā-Billāh. Wâlā Tâḥzân [c]Alâyhim-Wâla-Tâkô-Fī-dâyqim-mimmā-Yâmkoroon. Innâl-lāhâ-Mâ[c]âl-lâthīnât-tâqâo Wâllâthinâ-Hom Muḥsinoon

(58)

Say: "Enough is Allah
For a witness between me
And you: for He is
Well acquainted with His servants,
And He sees (all things).
(17:96)

قُلۡ كَفَىٰ بِٱللَّهِ شَهِيدَۢا بَيۡنِي وَبَيۡنَكُمۡۚ
إِنَّهُۥ كَانَ بِعِبَادِهِۦ خَبِيرَۢا بَصِيرٗا ٩٦

Qul-Kâfā-Billāhi-Shâheedâm-Bâynī-Wâbâynâkum Innâho-Kānâ-Bi[c]ibādihī Khâbeerâm-Bâṣeera

(59)

"No reason have we why
We should not put our trust
On Allah. Indeed He
Has guided us to the Ways
We (follow). We shall certainly
Bear with patience all
The hurt you may cause us.
For those who put their trust
Should put their trust on Allah."
(14:12)

وَمَا لَنَآ أَلَّا نَتَوَكَّلَ عَلَى ٱللَّهِ وَقَدۡ هَدَىٰنَا
سُبُلَنَاۚ وَلَنَصۡبِرَنَّ عَلَىٰ مَآ ءَاذَيۡتُمُونَاۚ وَعَلَى ٱللَّهِ
فَلۡيَتَوَكَّلِ ٱلۡمُتَوَكِّلُونَ ١٢

Wâmā-Lânā-Allā-Nâtâwâkkâlâ-[c]Alâl-lāhi-wâqâd-Hâdānā-Subulânā Wâlânâṣbirânnâ-[c]Alā-Mā Āthâytomoonā Wâ[c]âlâl-lāhi-Fâlyâtâwâkkâlil-Mutâwâkkiloon

E. Seeking Provisions

(60)

"O my Lord!
Truly am I
In (desperate) need
Of any good
That Thou dost send me!"...

رَبِّ إِنِّي لِمَآ أَنزَلْتَ إِلَيَّ مِنْ خَيْرٍ فَقِيرٌ ﴿٢٤﴾

(28:24)

Râbbî-innî-Lîmā-Anzâltâ-ilâyyâ-Min-Khâyrin-Fâqeer

(61)

"O my Lord!
Expand me my breast;

رَبِّ ٱشْرَحْ لِى صَدْرِى ﴿٢٥﴾

"Ease my task for me;

وَيَسِّرْ لِىٓ أَمْرِى ﴿٢٦﴾

"And remove the impediment
From my speech,

وَٱحْلُلْ عُقْدَةً مِّن لِّسَانِى ﴿٢٧﴾

"So they may understand
What I say:

يَفْقَهُوا۟ قَوْلِى ﴿٢٨﴾

(20:25-28)

Râbbish-râḥ-lî-ṣâdrî Wâyâssir-Lî-Amrî Wâhlol ᶜoqdâtâm-mil-Lisāni-yâfqâhoo-Qâwlî

III. Seeking Protection of Allah

(62)

"Glory to Thee!
Our (tie) is with Thee—
As Protector —not with them.
(34:41)

سُبْحَٰنَكَ أَنتَ وَلِيُّنَا مِن دُونِهِم

Subḥānâkâ-Antâ-Wâliyyonā-Min-Doonihim

(63)

Allah sufficeth me:
There is no god but He:
On Him is my trust,—
He the Lord of the Throne
(Of Glory) Supreme!"
(9:129)

حَسْبِيَ ٱللَّهُ لَآ إِلَٰهَ إِلَّا هُوَ عَلَيْهِ
تَوَكَّلْتُ وَهُوَ رَبُّ ٱلْعَرْشِ ٱلْعَظِيمِ ﴿١٢٩﴾

Ḥâsbiyâl-lāho-Lā-Ilāhâ-Illāho. ^{c}Alâyhi-Tâwâkkâltô-Wâhowâ-Râbbol ^{c}arshil-^{c}âẓeem

(64)

"O my Lord!
I do seek refuge with Thee,
Lest I ask Thee for that
Of which I have no knowledge.
And unless Thou forgive me
And have Mercy on me,
I should indeed be lost!"
(11:47)

رَبِّ إِنِّيٓ أَعُوذُ بِكَ أَنْ أَسْـَٔلَكَ مَا لَيْسَ
لِى بِهِۦ عِلْمٌ وَإِلَّا تَغْفِرْ لِى وَتَرْحَمْنِىٓ أَكُن
مِّنَ ٱلْخَٰسِرِينَ ﴿٤٧﴾

Râbbi-Innī-A^{c}ootho-Bikâ-An-As'âlâkâ-Mā-Lysâ Lī-Bihī-^{c}Ilm Wâillā-Tâghfir-li-Wâtâr-ḥâmnī-Akom-Minâl-Khāsireen

(65)

But Allah is the best
To take care (of him),
And He is the Most Merciful
Of those who show mercy!"
(12:64)

فَٱللَّهُ خَيْرٌ حَٰفِظًا وَهُوَ أَرْحَمُ ٱلرَّٰحِمِينَ ﴿٦٤﴾

Fâllāho-Khâyron-Ḥāfiẓa. Wâhowâ-Arḥâmor-rāḥimeen

(66)

And say "O my Lord!
I seek refuge with Thee
From the suggestions
Of the Evil Ones.

وَقُل رَّبِّ أَعُوذُ بِكَ مِنْ هَمَزَٰتِ ٱلشَّيَٰطِينِ ﴿٩٧﴾

"And I seek refuge with Thee
O my Lord! lest they
Should come near me."

وَأَعُوذُ بِكَ رَبِّ أَن يَحْضُرُونِ ﴿٩٨﴾

(23:97-98)

Wâqul-Râbbi-A[c]oothô-Bikâ-Min-Hâmâzātish-shâyāṭeen. Wâ'a[c]oothô Bikâ-râbbî-Ay-Yâḥḍoroon

(67)

Creator of the heavens
And the earth! Thou art
My Protector in this world
And in the Hereafter.
Take Thou my soul (at death)
As one submitting to Thy Will
(As a Muslim), and unite me
With the righteous."

فَاطِرَ ٱلسَّمَٰوَٰتِ وَٱلْأَرْضِ
أَنتَ وَلِىِّۦ فِى ٱلدُّنْيَا وَٱلْءَاخِرَةِ ۖ تَوَفَّنِى
مُسْلِمًا وَأَلْحِقْنِى بِٱلصَّٰلِحِينَ ﴿١٠١﴾

(12:101)

Fāṭirâs-sâmāwâti-Wâlarḍi-Antâ-Wâliȳyī-Fid-donyā-Wâl'ākhirâh. Tâwâffânī-Muslimâw-wâ'âlḥiqni-Biṣṣāliheen

(68)

"Our Lord!
Avert from us the Wrath
Of Hell, for its Wrath
Is indeed an affliction grievous,—

رَبَّنَا ٱصْرِفْ عَنَّا عَذَابَ
جَهَنَّمَ ۖ إِنَّ عَذَابَهَا كَانَ غَرَامًا ﴿٦٥﴾

(25:65)

Râbbânâṣrif-[c]Annā-[c]âthābâ-Jâhânnâm-Innâ [c]âthābâhā-Kānâ-Ghârāmā

(69)

"In Allah Do we put our trust. Our Lord! make us not A trial for those Who practise oppression:	عَلَى ٱللَّهِ تَوَكَّلْنَا رَبَّنَا لَا تَجْعَلْنَا فِتْنَةً لِّلْقَوْمِ ٱلظَّٰلِمِينَ ﴿٨٥﴾
"And deliver us by Thy Mercy From those who reject (Thee)."	وَنَجِّنَا بِرَحْمَتِكَ مِنَ ٱلْقَوْمِ ٱلْكَٰفِرِينَ ﴿٨٦﴾

(10:85-86)

cÂlâl-Lāhi-Tâwakkalnā. Rabbânā-Lā Taj^{c}âlnā Fitnatal-Lilqâwmiẓ-ẓālimeen. Wanajjinā Berâḥmâtikâ-Minâl-qâwmil-Kāfireen

(70)

In the name of Allah, Most Gracious, Most Merciful.	بِسْمِ ٱللَّهِ ٱلرَّحْمَٰنِ ٱلرَّحِيمِ
1. Say: I seek refuge With the Lord of the Dawn,	قُلْ أَعُوذُ بِرَبِّ ٱلْفَلَقِ ﴿١﴾
2. From the mischief Of created things;	مِن شَرِّ مَا خَلَقَ ﴿٢﴾
3. From the mischief Of Darkness as it overspreads;	وَمِن شَرِّ غَاسِقٍ إِذَا وَقَبَ ﴿٣﴾
4. From the mischief Of those who practise Secret Arts	وَمِن شَرِّ ٱلنَّفَّٰثَٰتِ فِى ٱلْعُقَدِ ﴿٤﴾
5. And from the mischief Of the envious one As he practises envy.	وَمِن شَرِّ حَاسِدٍ إِذَا حَسَدَ ﴿٥﴾

(113:1-5)

Bismillāhir-râḥmānir-râḥeem

1. Qul-â^{c}oothô-Birâbbil-Fâlâq 2. Min shârrî-MāKhâlâq 3. Wâmin-shârrî-ghāsiqin-Ithā Wâqâb 4. Wâmin-Shârrin-nâffāthātî-fîl-^{c}ôqâd 5. Wâmin shârrî-Ḥāsidin-Ithā-Ḥâsâd

In the name of Allah, Most Gracious, Most Merciful.	بِسْمِ اللَّهِ الرَّحْمَٰنِ الرَّحِيمِ
1. Say: I seek refuge With the Lord And Cherisher of Mankind,	قُلْ أَعُوذُ بِرَبِّ ٱلنَّاسِ ١
2. The King (or Ruler) Of Mankind,	مَلِكِ ٱلنَّاسِ ٢
3. The God (or Judge) Of Mankind,—	إِلَٰهِ ٱلنَّاسِ ٣
4. From the mischief Of the Whisperer (Of Evil), who withdraws (After his whisper)—	مِن شَرِّ ٱلْوَسْوَاسِ ٱلْخَنَّاسِ ٤
5. (The same) who whispers Into the hearts of Mankind,—	ٱلَّذِى يُوَسْوِسُ فِى صُدُورِ ٱلنَّاسِ ٥
6. Among Jinns And among Men.	مِنَ ٱلْجِنَّةِ وَٱلنَّاسِ ٦

(114:1-6)

Bismillāhir-râḥmānir-râḥeem

1. Qul-Aâ^{c}oothô-Birâbin-nās 2. Mâlîkîn-nās 3. Ilāhin-nās 4. Min-shârril-Wâswāsil-Khânnās 5. Allathī-Yuwâswîsô-Fī-Ṣudūrîn-nās 6. Minâl-Jinnâtî-Wânnās

IV. Offering of Thanks

(72)

Nay, but worship Allah,
And be of those who
Give thanks.
(39:66)

بَلِ ٱللَّهَ فَٱعۡبُدۡ وَكُن مِّنَ ٱلشَّٰكِرِينَ ﴿٦٦﴾

Bâlîl-lāhâ-Fâ^{c}bod-Wâkum-minâsh-shākireen

(73)

"This is
By the grace of my Lord!—
To test me whether I am
Grateful or ungrateful!
And if any is grateful,
Truly his gratitude is (a gain)
For his own soul; but if
Any is ungrateful, truly
My Lord is Free of all Needs,
Supreme in Honour!"
(27:40)

هَٰذَا مِن فَضۡلِ رَبِّي لِيَبۡلُوَنِيٓ ءَأَشۡكُرُ أَمۡ أَكۡفُرُۖ
وَمَن شَكَرَ فَإِنَّمَا يَشۡكُرُ لِنَفۡسِهِۦۖ
وَمَن كَفَرَ فَإِنَّ رَبِّي غَنِيّٞ كَرِيمٞ ﴿٤٠﴾

Hāthā-Min-Fâdlî-Râbbi-Liŷâblowâni-A'ashkurô-Âm Akfor. Wâmân Shâkârâ-Fi'innâmā-Yâshkuru-Linâfsih. Wâmân-Kâfârâ-Fi'innâ-Râbbī-Ghâniyyon-kâreem.

(74)

Then Praise be to Allah,
Lord of the heavens
And Lord of the earth,—
Lord and Cherisher
Of all the worlds!

فَلِلَّهِ ٱلۡحَمۡدُ رَبِّ ٱلسَّمَٰوَٰتِ وَرَبِّ ٱلۡأَرۡضِ
رَبِّ ٱلۡعَٰلَمِينَ ﴿٣٦﴾

To Him be Glory
Thoughout the heavens
And the earth: and He
Is Exalted in Power,
Full of Wisdom!
(45:36-37)

وَلَهُ ٱلۡكِبۡرِيَآءُ فِي ٱلسَّمَٰوَٰتِ وَٱلۡأَرۡضِۖ
وَهُوَ ٱلۡعَزِيزُ ٱلۡحَكِيمُ ﴿٣٧﴾

Fâlillāhil-ḥâmdu-Râbbis-sâmāwāti-Warabbil-ạrdị̂-Râbbil-^{c}ālâmeen. Wâlâhol-kibriā'o-Fis-samāwāti-Walard. Wâhowâl-^{c}âzizul-ḥâkeem

(75)

"Praise be to Allah,
Who hath guided us
To this (felicity): never
Could we have found
Guidance, had it not been
For the guidance of Allah:
(7:43)

ٱلْحَمْدُ لِلَّهِ ٱلَّذِى هَدَىٰنَا لِهَٰذَا
وَمَا كُنَّا لِنَهْتَدِىَ لَوْلَآ أَنْ هَدَىٰنَا ٱللَّهُ

Alḥâmdu-lillāhil-lathi-Hadānā-Lihāthā Wamā-Kunnā-Linâhtadiyâ-Lâolā-An-Hadānal-Lāh.

(76)

And He is Allah: there is
No god but He. To Him
Be praise, at the first
And at the last:
For Him is the Command,
And to Him shall ye
(All) be brought back.
(28:70)

وَهُوَ ٱللَّهُ لَآ إِلَٰهَ إِلَّا هُوَ لَهُ ٱلْحَمْدُ فِى ٱلْأُولَىٰ
وَٱلْءَاخِرَةِ وَلَهُ ٱلْحُكْمُ وَإِلَيْهِ تُرْجَعُونَ ﴿٧٠﴾

Wahowallāho-Lā-ilāha-Illāhu. Lahol-ḥâmdo-fil-oolā-Wâlākhirâh.
Walahol-ḥukmu-Wa'ilayhi-Turjâ[c]oon

V. Prayers For Family

(77)

"O my Lord! leave me not
Without offspring, though Thou
Art the best of inheritors."

(21:89)

رَبِّ لَا تَذَرْنِي فَرْدًا وَأَنتَ خَيْرُ الْوَارِثِينَ ﴿٨٩﴾

Râbbîlā-TâthârnīFârdâw-wa'antâ-Khâyrul-wāritheen

(78)

"O my Lord! grant me
A righteous (son)!"

(37:100)

رَبِّ هَبْ لِي مِنَ الصَّالِحِينَ ﴿١٠٠﴾

Râbbîhâbli-Mînâṣṣāliḥeen

(79)

"O my Lord! Grant unto me
From Thee a progeny
That is pure: for Thou
Art He that heareth prayer!

(3:38)

رَبِّ هَبْ لِي
مِن لَّدُنكَ ذُرِّيَّةً طَيِّبَةً إِنَّكَ سَمِيعُ الدُّعَاءِ ﴿٣٨﴾

Râbbihâbli-Millâdonkâ-Thurriyyâtân-Ṭâyyibâtâh. Innâkâ-Sâmī-ᶜuddûᶜā'

(80)

"Our Lord! Grant unto us
Wives and offspring who will be
The comfort of our eyes,
And give us (the grace)
To lead the righteous."

(25:74)

رَبَّنَا هَبْ لَنَا مِنْ أَزْوَاجِنَا
وَذُرِّيَّاتِنَا قُرَّةَ أَعْيُنٍ وَاجْعَلْنَا
لِلْمُتَّقِينَ إِمَامًا ﴿٧٤﴾

Râbbânā-Hâb-Lânā-Min-Azwājinā-wâthurriyyātinā-Qurrâtâ-aᶜyoniw-Wâjᶜalnā-Lilmuttâqeenâ-Imāmā

(81)

"Our Lord! make of us
Muslims, bowing to Thy (Will),
And of our progeny a people
Muslim, bowing to Thy (Will);
And show us our places for
The celebration of (due) rites;
And turn unto us (in Mercy);
For Thou art the Oft-Returning,
Most Merciful.

رَبَّنَا وَٱجْعَلْنَا مُسْلِمَيْنِ لَكَ وَمِن ذُرِّيَّتِنَآ أُمَّةً
مُّسْلِمَةً لَّكَ وَأَرِنَا مَنَاسِكَنَا وَتُبْ عَلَيْنَآ
إِنَّكَ أَنتَ ٱلتَّوَّابُ ٱلرَّحِيمُ ﴿١٢٨﴾

(2:128)

Râbbânā-Wâj^{c}alnā-Muslimynî-Lâkâ-Wâmin-Thurriyâtînā Ommâtâm-Muslimâtâl-Lâkâ-W'arîna-Mânāsîkânā-Wâtub^{c}Alâynā-Innâkâ-Antât-tâwwābur-râḥeem

(82)

"O my Lord! make me
One who establishes regular Prayer,
And also (raise such)
Among my offspring
O our Lord!
And accept Thou my Prayer.

رَبِّ ٱجْعَلْنِى مُقِيمَ ٱلصَّلَوٰةِ وَمِن ذُرِّيَّتِى
رَبَّنَا وَتَقَبَّلْ دُعَآءِ ﴿٤٠﴾

"O our Lord! cover (us)
With Thy Forgiveness—me,
My parents, and (all) Believers,—
On the Day that the Reckoning
Will be established!

رَبَّنَا ٱغْفِرْ لِى وَلِوَٰلِدَىَّ وَلِلْمُؤْمِنِينَ يَوْمَ يَقُومُ
ٱلْحِسَابُ ﴿٤١﴾

(14:40-41)

Râbbij^{c}âlni-Muqeemâs-ṣâlātî-wâmin-thurriyyâti. Râbbâna-wātâqâbbâl-Du^{c}ā'. Râbbâna-gh-firli Wâliwālidâyyâ-Wâlilmu'mineenâ-Yâwmâ-Yâqoom-ol-ḥisāb

(83)

"O my Lord!
Grant me that I may be
Grateful for Thy favour
Which Thou hast bestowed
Upon me, and upon both
My parents, and that I
May work righteousness
Such as Thou mayest approve;
And be gracious to me
In my issue. Truly
Have I turned to Thee
And truly do I bow
(To Thee) in Islam."
(46:15)

رَبِّ أَوۡزِعۡنِيٓ أَنۡ أَشۡكُرَ نِعۡمَتَكَ ٱلَّتِيٓ أَنۡعَمۡتَ عَلَيَّ
وَعَلَىٰ وَٰلِدَيَّ وَأَنۡ أَعۡمَلَ صَٰلِحٗا تَرۡضَىٰهُ
وَأَصۡلِحۡ لِي فِي ذُرِّيَّتِيٓۖ إِنِّي تُبۡتُ إِلَيۡكَ وَإِنِّي
مِنَ ٱلۡمُسۡلِمِينَ ١٥

Râbbî'awzi^{c}nī-Ân-Ashkôrâ-Ni^{c}mâtâkâl-lâtī-An^{c}amtâ-^{c}Alâyyâ-Wâ^{c}âla–Wālidâyyâ-Wâ'ân A^{c}mâlâ-Ṣālihân-Târḍāho-Wâ'aṣliḥ-li-Fī-Thurriyyâtī. Innī Tubtû-Ilâykâ-Wâ'innī Minâl-muslimeen

(84)

"My Lord! bestow on them
Thy Mercy even as they
Cherished me in childhood."
(17:24)

رَّبِّ ٱرۡحَمۡهُمَا كَمَا رَبَّيَانِي صَغِيرٗا ٢٤

Râbbîr-ḥâmḥomā-Kâmā-Râbbâyāni-Ṣâgheerā

(85)

"O my Lord! Forgive me,
My parents, all who
Enter my house in Faith,
And (all) believing men
And believing women:
And to the wrong-doers
Grant Thou no increase
But in Perdition!"
(71:28)

رَّبِّ ٱغۡفِرۡ لِي وَلِوَٰلِدَيَّ وَلِمَن دَخَلَ بَيۡتِيَ
مُؤۡمِنٗا وَلِلۡمُؤۡمِنِينَ وَٱلۡمُؤۡمِنَٰتِۖ وَلَا تَزِدِ ٱلظَّٰلِمِينَ
إِلَّا تَبَارَۢا ٢٨

Râbbigh-fir-li-Wâliwālidâyyâ-Wâlimân-Dâkhâlâ-Bâytiyâ Mu'minâw-wâlilmu'mineenâ-Wâl-mu'minātî-Wâlā-tâzidiẓ-ẓālimeenâ-illā-Tâbārā

VI. General

(86)

"Our Lord! Give us
Good in this world
And good in the Hereafter,
And defend us
From the torment
Of the Fire!"
(2:201)

رَبَّنَآ ءَاتِنَا فِى ٱلدُّنْيَا
حَسَنَةً وَفِى ٱلْـَٔاخِرَةِ حَسَنَةً وَقِنَا عَذَابَ
ٱلنَّارِ ﴿٢٠١﴾

Râbbânā-Ātinā-Fid-donyā-Ḥâsântâw-wâfil-Ākhirâtî-Hâsânâtâw-wâqîinā-^{c}Athābân-nār.

(87)

"And ordain for us
That which is good,
In this life
And in the Hereafter:
For we have turned unto Thee."
(7:156)

۞ وَٱكْتُبْ لَنَا فِى هَٰذِهِ ٱلدُّنْيَا حَسَنَةً وَفِى
ٱلْـَٔاخِرَةِ إِنَّا هُدْنَآ إِلَيْكَ

Wâktob-Lânā-Fi-hāthîhîd-donyā-Hâsânâtâw-wâfil-Ākhirâtî-Innā-Hodnā-Ilaŷk.

(88)

"We should indeed invent
A lie against Allah,
If we returned to your ways
After Allah hath rescued
Us therefrom; nor could we
By any manner of means
Return thereto unless it be
As in the will and plan of Allah,
Our Lord. Our Lord
Can reach out to the utmost
Recesses of things by His knowledge.
In Allah is our trust.
Our Lord! Decide thou
Between us and our people
In truth, for thou
Art the best to decide."
(7:89)

قَدِ ٱفْتَرَيْنَا عَلَى ٱللَّهِ كَذِبًا إِنْ عُدْنَا فِى مِلَّتِكُم
بَعْدَ إِذْ نَجَّىٰنَا ٱللَّهُ مِنْهَا وَمَا يَكُونُ لَنَآ أَن نَّعُودَ فِيهَآ
إِلَّآ أَن يَشَآءَ ٱللَّهُ رَبُّنَا وَسِعَ رَبُّنَا كُلَّ شَىْءٍ عِلْمًا
عَلَى ٱللَّهِ تَوَكَّلْنَا رَبَّنَا ٱفْتَحْ بَيْنَنَا وَبَيْنَ قَوْمِنَا
بِٱلْحَقِّ وَأَنتَ خَيْرُ ٱلْفَٰتِحِينَ ﴿٨٩﴾

Qâdif-târâynā-^{c}Âlâl-Lahi-Kâthîban-In-^{c}Odnā Fī-Millâtikum-Bâ^{c}dâ-Ith-Nâjjānâl-Lāhô-Minhā. Wâmā-Yâkoonô-Lânā-Ân-Nâ^{c}odâ-Fīhā-Illā-Ay-Yâshā'â-Râbonā. Wâsi^{c}â-Râbbonā-Kullâ-Shây'in^{c}Ilmā. ^{c}âlâl-lāhî-tâwâkkâlnā. Râbbânâf-tâḥ-Bâynâna-Wâbâynâ-qâwminā-Bilḥâqqi-Wâ'ântâ-Khâyrul-Fātiheen.

(89)

"Our Lord! Thy Reach
Is over all things,
In Mercy and Knowledge.
Forgive, then, those who
Turn in Repentance, and follow
Thy Path; and preserve them
From the Penalty
Of the Blazing Fire!

رَبَّنَا وَسِعْتَ كُلَّ شَيْءٍ رَّحْمَةً وَعِلْمًا
فَٱغْفِرْ لِلَّذِينَ تَابُوا۟ وَٱتَّبَعُوا۟ سَبِيلَكَ
وَقِهِمْ عَذَابَ ٱلْجَحِيمِ ﴿٧﴾

"And grant, our Lord!
That they enter
The Gardens of Eternity,
Which Thou hast promised
To them, and to the righteous
Among their fathers,
Their wives, and their posterity!
For Thou art (He),
The Exalted in Might,
Full of Wisdom.

رَبَّنَا وَأَدْخِلْهُمْ جَنَّٰتِ عَدْنٍ ٱلَّتِى وَعَدتَّهُمْ
وَمَن صَلَحَ مِنْ ءَابَآئِهِمْ وَأَزْوَٰجِهِمْ
وَذُرِّيَّٰتِهِمْ ۚ إِنَّكَ أَنتَ ٱلْعَزِيزُ ٱلْحَكِيمُ ﴿٨﴾

"And preserve them
From (all) ills;
And any whom Thou
Dost preserve from ills
That Day,—on them
Wilt Thou have bestowed
Mercy indeed: and that
Will be truly (for them)
The highest Achievement"

وَقِهِمُ ٱلسَّيِّـَٔاتِ ۚ وَمَن تَقِ ٱلسَّيِّـَٔاتِ يَوْمَئِذٍ
فَقَدْ رَحِمْتَهُۥ ۚ وَذَٰلِكَ هُوَ ٱلْفَوْزُ ٱلْعَظِيمُ ﴿٩﴾

(40:7-9)

Râbbânā-Wâs̱î^{c}tâ-Kullâ-Shây'ir-Râẖmâtâw-Wâ^{c}ilma-Fâghfîr-Lîllâtheenâ-Tābū-Wâttâbâ^{c}oo-Sâbilâkâ-Wâqîẖîm-^{c}Aẓābal-Jâḥeem
Râbbânā-Wa'adkhilhom-Jânnāti-^{c}âdinin-il-lâti-Wâ^{c}âdtâhom-Wâm̱ân-Ṣâlâhâ-Min-Ābā'ihim Wâ'azwājihim-Wâthorriyyātihim. Innâkâ-Antâl-^{c}âzizul-ḥâkeem.
Wâqihimus-sâyyi'āt. Wâmân-Tâqis-sâyyi'ātî-Yâwmâ'ithin-Fâqâd-Râhimtâh. Wâthālikâ-Howâl-Fâwzul-^{c}Âẓeem

Chapter Two

Du^cā' From Sunnah Al-Ma'thoorāt

(90)

أَصْبَحْنَا وَأَصْبَحَ الْمُلْكُ لِلَّهِ وَالْحَمْدُ لِلَّهِ لا شَرِيكَ
لَهُ ، لَا إِلَٰهَ إِلَّا هُوَ وَإِلَيْهِ النُّشُورُ (ثلاثا).

Aṣbâḥnā wa'aṣbâḥâl-mulkû lillāh. Wâlhâmdul-illāh. La Sharikâ Lâh. Lā Ilahâ Illā howâ Wâ'ilây-hin-nushure.

We rose up in the morning and so does the domain of Allāh's. Grace is due to Him, He has no partner. There is no deity but Him, unto Whom is the return. (3 times)

(91)

أَصْبَحْنَا عَلَى فِطْرَةِ الْإِسْلَامِ ، وَكَلِمَةِ الْإِخْلَاصِ
وَعَلَى دِينِ نَبِيِّنَا مُحَمَّدٍ صلى اللهُ عليهِ وَسلّم ، وَعَلَى مِلَّةِ أَبِينَا
إِبْرَاهِيمَ حَنِيفاً (١) وَمَا كَانَ مِنَ الْمُشْرِكِينَ (ثلاثا)

Asbâḥnā ^{c}âlā Fiṭrâtil-Islām. Wâkâlimâtil-Ikhlās. Wâ^{c}âlā deeni nâbiyyinā Muḥâmmâdin Ṣâllâl-Lâho ^{c}Alâyhi Wâsâllâm. Wâ^{c}alā Millâtî Abīnā Ibrāhimâ hânifâw-wâmā Kānâ Minâl-Mushrikeen

Chapter Three

Daily Duʿā'

We rose up with innate nature of Al-Islām, and with the word of purity (Ikhlās), and on the deen (way of life) of our Prophet Muhâmmâd (S.A.W.), and on the deen of our father Ibrāhim, the upright (in truth) who was not of the Mushriks (associators of other deities with Allāh).
(3 times)

(92)

اللّٰهُمَّ إنِّى أَصْبَحْتُ مِنْكَ فى نِعْمَةٍ وَعافِيَةٍ وَسِتْرٍ ،
فَأَتِمَّ عَلَىَّ نِعْمَتَكَ وَعافِيَتَكَ وَسِتْرَكَ فِى الدُّنْيا
وَالآخِرَةِ (ثلاثاً).

Allāhommâ Inni. Aṣbâḥtô minkâ Fị-Ni^{c}mâtiw-wâ^{c}āfiyâtiw Wâsâtr.
Fâ'atimmâ ^{c}âlâyyâ ni^{c} mâtâkâ Wâ^{c}āfiyâtâkâ Wâsitrâkâ
Fid-donyā-Wâl-ākhirâh

O Allāh! I rose up in the morning with blessings, strength, and concealment (of my deficiencies), all from You. So complete all the blessings and strength from you and the concealment for me in this life and in the hereafter.

(93)

اللّٰهُمَّ مَا أَصْبَحَ بِي مِن نِعْمَةٍ أَوْ بِأَحَدٍ مِنْ خَلْقِكَ فَمِنْكَ وَحْدَكَ لَا شَرِيكَ لَكَ ، فَلَكَ الْحَمْدُ ، وَلَكَ الشُّكْرُ (ثلاثاً)

Allāhommâ mā aṣbâḥâ bi min ni^{c}mâtin Ao bi'aḥadin min Khâlkhikâ fâminkâ Wâḥdak. Lā Shârikâ Lâk. Fâlâkâl-ḥâmdu-Wâlâkâsh-Shukr

O Allāh! Whatever blessings I or any of Your creatures rose up with, is only from You, You have no partner, so all grace and thanks are due to You.
(3 times)

(94)

يَا رَبِّ لَكَ الْحَمْدُ كَمَا يَنْبَغِي لِجَلَالِ وَجْهِكَ وَعَظِيمِ سُلْطَانِكَ (ثلاثاً).

Yā râbbi Lâkâl-ḥâmdu Kâmā Yânbâghi Lijâlālî Wâjhikâ Wâ^{c}Âẓeemî Sulṭānik

O my Lord! All Grace is due to You which is befitting to Your glorious presence and Your great sovereignty.
(3 times)

(95)

رَضِيتُ بِاللهِ رَبًّا ، وَبِالإِسْلَامِ دِينًا ، وَبِمُحَمَّدٍ نَبِيًّا وَرَسُولًا (ثلاثًا).

Râḍitô biLLāhî Râbba · Wâbil-Islāmî đînâ.
Wâbimuḥâmmâdin-nâbiyyâw-wârâsūla.

I have accepted Allāh for Lord, Al-Islām for way of life, and Muhâmmâd as Prophet and messenger (of Allāh).
(3 times)

(96)

سُبْحَانَ اللهِ وَبِحَمْدِهِ ، عَدَدَ خَلْقِهِ وَرِضَا نَفْسِهِ ، وَزِنَةَ عَرْشِهِ ، وَمِدَادَ كَلِمَاتِهِ (ثلاثًا).

Ṣubḥânâl-Lāhi Wâbiḥâmdihi ᶜâdâdâ Khâl-qihi Wâriḍā nâfsihi Wâzinâtâ ᶜârshihi Wâmidâdâ Kâlimātih

Glory be to Allāh and grace is His (as great as) the number of His creatures, the extent of His satisfaction, the weight of his domain, and the ink (needed to write down His countless) signs (of presence, omnipotence, and grace)

(97)

بِسْمِ اللهِ الَّذِى لا يَضُرُّ مَعَ اسْمِهِ شَىْءٌ فِى الأَرْضِ
وَلاَ فِى السَّمَاءِ وَهُوَ السَّمِيعُ الْعَلِيمُ (ثلاثاً.)

Bîsmîllāhîl-Lâṯẖī L̲ā yâḍorrô mâ^{c}âsmihi Shây'on Fil-arḍi Wâlā fis-sâmā'i wâhowâs-sâmi^{c}ul^{c}âlīm.

In the name of Allāh, with Whose name nothing in earth or in heavens can hurt, and He is the Hearer, the Knower.
(3 times)

(98)

اللَّهُمَّ إِنَّا نَعُوذُ بِكَ مِنْ أَنْ نُشْرِكَ بِكَ شَيْئاً
نَعلَمُهُ، وَنَسْتَغْفِرُكَ لِمَا لاَ نَعْلَمُه (ثلاثاً.)

All̲āhommâ Innā Nâ^{c}oothô Bîkâ Min An Nushrikâ Bîkâ Shây'ân Nâ^{c}Lâmoh. Wânâstâgh-firôkâ Līmā Lā Nâ^{c}Lâmoh

O Allāh! We seek Your refuge from knowingly associating others with You and we seek Your forgiveness from associating others with You unknowingly.
(3 times)

(99)

أَعُوذُ بِكَلِمَاتِ اللهِ التَّامَّاتِ مِنْ شَرِّ مَا خَلَقَ

(ثلاثاً)

Â^{c}oothô bîkâlimātîl-lāhit-tāmmātî-min shârrî mā Khâlâq

I seek refuge in the Perfect words of Allāh from any evil creature.
(3 times)

(100)

اللَّهُمَّ إِنِّى أَعُوذُ بِكَ مِنَ الْهَمِّ وَالْحَزَنِ ، وَأَعُوذُ
بِكَ مِنَ الْعَجْزِ وَالْكَسَلِ ، وَأَعُوذُ بِكَ مِنَ الْجُبْنِ
وَالْبُخْلِ ، وَأَعُوذُ بِكَ مِنْ غَلَبَةِ الدَّيْنِ وَقَهْرِ الرِّجَالِ (ثلاثاً)

Allāhommâ inni â^{c}oothô bîkâ minâl-hâmmî-wâlhâzân. Wâ'a^{c}oothô bîkâ-minâl-ghâmmî-wâl-kâsâl. Wa'a^{c}oothô-bîkâ-minâl Jubnî wâl bukhl. Wa'a^{c}oothô-bîkâ min ghâlâbâtid-dâynî-Wâqâhrir-rijāl.

O Allāh! I seek refuge in You from worry and grief, from helplessness and laziness, from cowardice and stinginess, and from overpowering of debt and from oppression of men.

(101)

اللّهُمَّ عَافِنِى فى بَدَنِى ، اللّهُمَّ عافِنِى فى سَمْعِى ،

اللّهُمَّ عافِنِى فى بَصَرِى (ثلاثاً ،)

Allāhomâ ^{c}āfini fi-bâdâni. Allāhommâ ^{c}āfini fi-sâm^{c}ī. Allāhommâ ^{c}āfini fi-bâṣarī.

O Allāh! Grant health to my body, to my hearing and to my sight.
(3 times)

(102)

اللّهُمَّ إنِّى أعُوذُ بِكَ

مِنَ الْكُفْرِ وَالْفَقْرِ ، اللّهُمَّ إنِّى أعُوذُ بِكَ مِنْ عذابِ

الْقَبْرِ ، لَا إلٰهَ إلّا أنْتَ (ثلاثاً)

Allāhommâ innī a^{c}ootho bikâ minâl-Kufrî Wâlfâqr. Allāhommâ inni â^{c}ootho bîkâ-min-^{c}âthābil-Qâbr. Lā-Ilāhâ-Illā'ant.

O Allāh! I seek refuge in You from unbelief and poverty. O Allāh! I seek refuge in You from punishment of the grave. There is no deity but You.
(3 times)

اللّهُمَّ أَنْتَ رَبِّى لَا إِلٰهَ إِلّا أنتَ ، خَلَقْتَنى وَأنا
عَبْدُكَ وَأنا عَلَى عَهْدِكَ وَوَعْدِكَ ما اسْتَطَعْتُ ، أعُوذُ بكَ
مِنْ شرِ مَا صَنَعْتُ ، أَبُوءُ لكَ بنِعْمَتِكَ عَلَيَّ وَأبُوءُ
بِذَنبِى فَاغفِرْ لِى فإنَّهُ لا يَغفِرُ الذُّنُوبَ إلَّا أنتَ (ثلاثاً)

Allāhommâ antâ râbbī Lā-ilāhâ illā'ânt. Khâlâkhtâni Wâ'ânâ ^{c}Âbdok W'ânâ ^{c}âlā ^{c}âhdikâ Wâwâ^{c}dikâ mâs-tâtâ^{c}t. Â^{c}oothô bīkâ min shârrî mā Ṣânâ^{c}t. Aboo'ô Lâkâ bini^{c}mâtikâ ^{c}Âlâyyâ Wa'boo'ô bithânbī fâghfirlī fâ'innâhō Lā Yâghfroth-thônoobâ-illā-ânt

O Allāh! You are my Lord, there is no deity but You. You created me and I am Your slave-servant. And I am trying my best to keep my oath (of faith) to You and to seek to live in the hope of Your promise. I seek refuge in You from my greatest-evil deeds. I acknowledge Your blessings upon me and I acknowledge my sins. So forgive me for none but You can forgive sins.
(3 times)

(104)

أَسْتَغْفِرُ اللهَ الَّذِى لَا إِلٰهَ إِلَّا هُوَ الْحَىَّ الْقَيُّومَ

وَأَتُوبُ إِلَيْهِ (ثلاثًا)

Astâgh-firol-lāhâl-Lâthi Lā ilāhâ illā howâl-hâyyâl-qâyyomâ w'atoobo ilâyh

I seek forgiveness from Allāh, there is no deity but Him, the Living, the Eternal and I repent to Him.
(3 times)

(105)

اللّهُمَّ صَلِّ عَلَى سَيِّدِنَا مُحَمَّدٍ وَعَلَى آلِ سَيِّدِنَا مُحَمَّدٍ

كَمَا صَلَّيْتَ عَلَى سَيِّدِنَا إِبْرَاهِيمَ وَعَلَى آلِ سَيِّدِنَا إِبْرَاهِيمَ

وَبَارِكْ عَلَى سَيِّدِنَا مُحَمَّدٍ وَعَلَى آلِ سَيِّدِنَا مُحَمَّدٍ كَمَا

بَارَكْتَ عَلَى سَيِّدِنَا إبراهِيمَ وَعَلَى آلِ سَيِّدِنَا إبراهِيمَ

فِى الْعَالَمِينَ ؛ إِنَّكَ حَمِيدٌ مَجِيدٌ (عَشْرًا)

Allāhommâ Ṣâlli ^{c}alā Muhâmmâdiw-Wâ^{c}âlā ālî Muhâmmâd. Kâmā Ṣâllâytâ ^{c}âlā Ibrāhîmâ wâ^{c}âlā ālî Ibrāhîm. Wâbārik ^{c}âlā Muhâmmâdiw-wâ^{c}âlā ālî Muḥâmmâd. Kâmā bārâktâ ^{c}âlā Ibrāhîmâ-Wâ^{c}âlā āli Ibrāhîm. Fil ^{c}ālâmina innâkâ ḥâmîdum mâjîd.

O Allāh! Have mercy on Muhâmmâd and on the progeny of Muhammad, as you had mercy on Ibrāhîm and the progeny of Ibrāhîm. And bless

Muhâmmâd and the progeny of Muhammad as you blessed Ibrāhim and the projeny of Ibrāhim in this universe. Indeed, you are Gracious, Glorious.
(10 times)

(106)

سُبْحَانَ اللهِ ، وَالحَمْدُ لِلهِ ، وَلَاإِلٰهَ إِلَّا اللهُ ، وَاللهُ أَكْبَرُ (مِائَة) .

Subḥānâl-llāh. Wâlḥâmdû-lillāh Wâlā-ilāhâ-illâl-lāh. Wâllāhô-Akbâr.

Glory be to Allāh, Grace is due to Allāh; there is no deity but Allāh and Allāh is The Great.
(100 times)

(107)

لَا إِلٰهَ إِلَّا اللهُ وَحْدَهُ لَا شَرِيكَ لَهُ ، لَهُ المُلْكُ وَلَهُ الحَمْدُ ، وَهُوَ عَلَى كُلِّ شَيْءٍ قَدِيرٌ (عشراً) .

Lā-ilāhâ-illâl-Lāh. Wâhdâhō Lā Shârikâ-Lâh. Lâhôl-Mulk. Wâlâhôl-ḥâmd. Wâhowâ ᶜâlā Kulli Shây'in Qâdîr

There is no Deity but Allāh alone. He has no partner. Sovereignty and grace are His; and He is Omnipotent.
(10 times)

(108)

سُبْحَانَكَ اللّهُمَّ وَبِحَمْدِكَ، أَشْهَدُ أَنْ لَا إِلٰهَ إِلَّا أَنْتَ،

أَسْتَغْفِرُكَ وَأَتُوبُ إِلَيْكَ (ثلاثا).

Subḥānâkâl-Lāhommâ Wâbiḥâmdik. Ash-hâdô Allā-ilāhâ-illā-ânt. Astâghfirokâ W'âtoobo-ilâyk.

Glory be to You, O Allāh, and all Praise! I testify there is no deity but You. I seek Your forgiveness and to You do I repent.
(3 times)

Daily Du^{c}ā'

Waking up

(109)

الْحَمْدُ لِلّٰهِ الَّذِي أَحْيَانَا بَعْدَ مَا أَمَاتَنَا وَإِلَيْهِ النُّشُورُ

Alhâmdû-lillāh-il-Lâthi Aḥyānā Bâ^{c}dâmā Amātânā Wa'ilâyhin-Nushūr.

Praise be to Allāh Who gave us life after death and unto Him will be the return.

When entering the bathroom

(110)

اللَّهُمَّ إِنِّي أَعُوذُ بِكَ مِنَ الْخُبْثِ وَالْخَبَائِثِ

Allāhommâ Innî A^{c}oothô Bîkâ Minâl Khubutḣî Wâl-khâbā'itḣ.

O Allāh! I seek refuge in You from male and female devils.

When leaving the bathroom

(111)

غُفْرَانَكَ

Ghufrānâk

I seek Your forgiveness (O Allāh!)

While making Wuḍū' (Ablution)

(112)

اَللّٰهُمَّ اغْفِرْ لِيْ ذَنْبِيْ وَوَسِّعْ لِيْ فِيْ دَارِيْ وَبَارِكْ لِيْ فِيْ رِزْقِيْ

Allāhommâ-gh-firli thânbi, Wâwâssi^c li Fi-dārī Wâbārik-li Fi-rizqi

O Allāh! Forgive my sins and expand (bless) my home, and bless my livelihood.

After Completing Wuḍū'

(113)

أَشْهَدُ أَنْ لَا إِلٰهَ إِلَّا اللهُ وَحْدَهُ لَا شَرِيكَ لَهُ، وَأَشْهَدُ أَنَّ مُحَمَّداً عَبْدُهُ وَرَسُولُهُ، اللّٰهُمَّ اجْعَلْنِي مِنَ التَّوَّابِينَ، وَاجْعَلْنِي مِنَ الْمُتَطَهِّرِينَ

Ash-hâdô Allā Ilahâ Illâl-lāh. Wâhdâho Lā Shârikâ Lâh. Wâ'ashhâdo Annâ Muḥâmmâdân ^cAbduhu Wârâsūluh. Allāhommâj ^calni Minât-Tâwwābīn. Wâj^calni Minâl Mutaṭahhirīn

I bear witness that there is no deity but Allāh. He is Alone. He has no partner. And I bear witness that Muhâmmâd is His servant and Messenger. O Allāh! Make me of those who are repentant and of those who purify themselves.

After Athān is completed

(114)

اللّهمّ ربّ هذه الدّعوة التّامّة ،
والصّلاة القائمة آت محمّدا الوسيلة والفضيلة ، وابعثه
مقاما محمودا الّذى وعدته

Allāhommâ Rabbâ Hāthihid-dâ^{c}wâtit-tāmmâh.
Wâṣṣâlātil-Qā'imâh. Ātî Muḥâmmâdân-il Wâsilâtâ Wal-Faḍîlâtâ.
Wâb^{c}âthhô Mâqāmân Mâhmūdân-il-Lâthīs Wa^{c}âdtâh.

O Allāh! Lord of this perfect Call and the Ṣalāh to be offered; grant Muhâmmâd the privilege (of interceding) and also the eminence. And resurrect him to the praised position You have promised.

When leaving the house

(115)

بسم الله توكّلت على الله ولا حول ولا قوّة إلّا بالله

Bismillāhi Tâwâkkâltû ^{c}Alâl-Lah. Lā Ḥaolâ Wâlā Qowwâtâ Illā Billāh.

In the name of Allāh. I depend on Allāh. There is no ability or power (for us) except by the leave of Allāh.

When going to the Mâsjid (Mosque)

(116)

اللَّهُمَّ اجْعَلْ فِي قَلْبِي نُورًا ، وَفِي بَصَرِي
نُورًا ، وَفِي سَمْعِي نُورًا ، وَعَنْ يَمِينِي نُورًا ، وَعَنْ يَسَارِي
نُورًا ، وَفَوْقِي نُورًا ، وَتَحْتِي نُورًا ، وَأَمَامِي نُورًا ،
وَخَلْفِي نُورًا ، وَاجْعَلْ لِي نُورًا

Allāhommâj-^{c}al Fī Qâlbi Noora Wâfī Bâsârī Noora. Wâfī Sam^{c}ī Noora. Wâ^{c}ân Yâmīnī Noora Wâ^{c}ân Yâsāri Noora. Wâfaoqī Noora. Wâtâḥtī Noora Wâ'amāmī Noora. Wâkhâlfi Noora. Wâj^{c}âl-li Noora.

O Allāh! Grant me light in my heart, light in my sight, light in my hearing, light to my right, light to my left, light above me, light underneath me, light before me, light behind me, and grant me light.

When entering the Mâsjid (Mosque):

(117)

بِسْمِ اللهِ اللَّهُمَّ صَلِّ عَلَى مُحَمَّدٍ اللَّهُمَّ افْتَحْ لِي أَبْوَابَ رَحْمَتِكَ

Bismillāh. Allāhommâ Ṣâllî ^{c}AlāMuḥâmmâd Allāhomâftâḥ-lī Abwābâ-râḥmâtik.

In the name of Allāh. O Allāh! Bless Muhâmmâd O Allāh! Open Your gates of mercy for me.

After completing (Ṣalāh)

(118)

مَنْ سَبَّحَ اللهَ فِي دُبُرِ كُلِّ
صَلَاةٍ ثَلَاثًا وَثَلَاثِينَ ، وَحَمِدَ اللهَ ثَلَاثًا وَثَلَاثِينَ ،
وَكَبَّرَ اللهَ ثَلَاثًا وَثَلَاثِينَ ، فَتِلْكَ تِسْعَةٌ وَتِسْعُونَ ،
وَقَالَ تَمَامَ الْمِائَةِ : لَا إِلٰهَ إِلَّا اللهُ وَحْدَهُ لَا شَرِيكَ لَهُ ، لَهُ
الْمُلْكُ وَلَهُ الْحَمْدُ وَهُوَ عَلَى كُلِّ شَيْءٍ قَدِيرٌ ، غُفِرَتْ
خَطَايَاهُ وَإِنْ كَانَتْ مِثْلَ زَبَدِ الْبَحْرِ

Note: Only the transliteration and translation of the actual du^{c}ā’ to be recited are included, not the full text of the ḥadeeth.

a. Subḥānâllāh (*Glory be to Allāh*) [33 times]
b. Alḥâmdulillāh (*Praise be to Allāh*) [33 times]
c. Allāhô-Akbâr (*Allāh is Great*) [33 times]
d. Lā Ilāhâ Illâl-Lāḥ. Wâḥdâhô Lā Shareeka Lâh. Lâhol-Mulk. Wâlâhol-Ḥâmd. Wâhowâ ^{c}Alā Kulli Shây’in Qâdîr

There is no deity but Allāh. He is Alone. He has no partner. His is the sovereignty and grace. And He is Omnipotent.

When leaving the masjid

(119)

اَللّٰهُمَّ إِنِّي أَسْأَلُكَ مِنْ فَضْلِكَ -

Allāhommâ Innî As’alokâ Min Fâḍlik

O Allāh! I beg of You Your bounty

When entering the house

(120)

اللّهُمَّ إِنِّي أَسْأَلُكَ خَيْرَ الْمَوْلِجِ
وَخَيْرَ الْمَخْرَجِ ، بِاسْمِ اللهِ وَلَجْنا ، وَ بِاسْمِ اللهِ خَرَجْنا
وَعَلَى اللهِ رَبِّنَا تَوَكَّلْنَا . ثُمَّ لِيُسَلِّمْ عَلَى أَهْلِهِ

Allāhommâ Innî As'alokâ Khâyrâl-Maolij. Wâkhâyrâl-Mâkhrâj. Bismillāhi Wâlâjnā Wâbismillāhi Khârâjnā Wâ[c]âlâl-Lāhi Râbbinā Tâwâkkâlnā

O Allāh! I ask you (to grant me) the best entering and the best exist. In the name of Allāh we entered, and in the name of Allāh we left, and upon Allāh, our Lord we depend.

When beginning the meal

(121)

اللّهُمَّ بَارِكْ لَنَا فِيمَا رَزَقْتَنَا ، وَقِنَا عَذَابَ النَّارِ ، بِسْمِ اللهِ

Allāhommâ Bārik Lânā Fîmā Râzâqtânā Wâqinā Athābân-Nār. Bismillāh

O Allāh! Bless (the food) You provided us and save us from the punishment of the hellfire. In the name of Allāh.

When finishing the meal:

(122)

اَلْحَمْدُ لِلّٰهِ الَّذِى أَطْعَمَنَا وَسَقَانَا وَجَعَلَنَا مُسْلِمِينَ

Alhâmdu-Lillāh-il Lâthi Aṭ^{c}amânā Wâsâqānā Wâjâ^{c}âlânā Muslimîn

Praise be to Allāh Who has fed us and given us drink, and made us Muslims.

When undressing:

(123)

بِسْمِ اللّٰهِ الَّذِى لَآ إِلٰهَ إِلَّا هُوَ

Bismillāh-il-lathi Lā Ilāhâ Illā Ho

In the name of Allāh. There is no deity save Him.

When getting dressed

(124)

اللَّهُمَّ إِنِّى أَسْأَلُكَ مِنْ خَيْرِهِ وَخَيْرِ مَا هُوَ لَهُ ، وَأَعُوذُ بِكَ
مِنْ شَرِّهِ وَشَرِّ مَا هُوَ لَهُ

Allāhommâ Innî As'alokâmin Khâyrihi Wâkhyrî-mā hôwâ Lâh. W'a^{c}oothô Bîkâ Min Shârrih Wâshârri-mā hôwâ Lâh.

O Allāh! I ask You the good in it and the good for which it is made. And I seek your protection from the evil in it and the evil for which it is made.

When mounting a means of transportation (horse, car, train, plane... etc.):

(125)

سُبْحَـٰنَ ٱلَّذِى سَخَّرَ لَنَا هَـٰذَا وَمَا كُنَّا لَهُۥ مُقْرِنِينَ

Subhānâl-Lâthī Sâkh-khârâ Lânā Hāthā. Wâmā Kunnā Lâhō Muqrineen. Wa'innā Ilā Râbbinā Lâmonqâliboon

Glory to Him Who has subjected these to our (use), for we could never have accomplished this (by ourselves). And to our Lord, surely must we turn back!

When retiring to sleep:

(126)

بِاسْمِكَ رَبِّي وَضَعْتُ جَنْبِي وَبِكَ أَرْفَعُهُ ، إِنْ أَمْسَكْتَ نَفْسِي فَاغْفِرْ لَهَا ، وَإِنْ أَرْسَلْتَهَا فَاحْفَظْهَا بِمَا تَحْفَظُ بِهِ عِبَادَكَ الصَّالِحِينَ » رواه الجماعة

Bismikâ Râbbī Wâḍa^c tô Jânbi Wâbīkâ Arfâ^c oh. Fâ'in Amsâktâ Nâfsī Fâghfir Lâhā. Wâ'in Arsâltâhā Fâḥfâẓhā Bīmā Tâḥfâẓo Bihi ^c Ībādâkâṣ-Ṣālihīn.

In Your Name, O Lord, I lay my side (to sleep). And by (Your leave) I raise it up. So if You take away my soul (during sleep) forgive it, and if You send it back (after sleep) protect it even as You protect Your pious servants.

I. In Personal Life

When looking in a mirror

(127)

اللّٰهُمَّ أَنتَ حَسَّنْتَ خَلْقِي فَحَسِّنْ خُلُقِي

وَحَرِّمْ وَجْهِي عَلَى النَّارِ ،

الْحَمْدُ لِلَّهِ الَّذِي سَوَّى خَلْقِي فَعَدَلَهُ ، وَكَرَّمَ صُورَةَ

وَجْهِي فَأَحْسَنَهَا وَجَعَلَنِي مِنَ الْمُسْلِمِينَ

Allāhommâ-antâ Ḥâssântâ Khâlqi Fâḥâssin Khulqi Waḥârrim Wâjhī ^{c}âlânnār. Alḥâmdu-lillāhî-llâthī Sâwwā Khâlqī fâ^{c}adâlâh Wâkârrâmâ Ṣoorâtâ-Wâjhī fa'aḥsânâhā. Wâjâ^{c}âlâni Minâl-muslimeen.

O Allāh! You made my physical constitution good so make my disposition good too and keep my face safe from the hellfire. Grace be to Allāh Who fashioned and made me proportionate, and honored my face and made me of the Muslims.

In case of insomnia

(128)

اللّٰهُمَّ رَبَّ السَّمٰوَاتِ السَّبْعِ

وَمَا أَظَلَّتْ وَرَبَّ الْأَرَضِينَ وَمَا أَقَلَّتْ وَرَبَّ الشَّيَاطِينِ

وَمَا أَضَلَّتْ كُنْ لِي جَارًا مِنْ شَرِّ خَلْقِكَ أَجْمَعِينَ أَنْ يَفْرُطَ

عَلَيَّ أَحَدٌ مِنْهُمْ أَوْ أَنْ يَطْغَى ، عَزَّ جَارُكَ ، وَتَبَارَكَ اسْمُكَ

Allāhomâ Râbbâs-Sâmāwātis-Sab^{c}i Wâmā Aẓâllât. Wârâbbâl-Arâḍinâ Wâmā Aqâllt̂ Wârâbbâsh-Shâyātīnâ Wâmā Aḍâllât Kun Li Jārân Min Shârri Khâlqikâ Ajmâ^{c}een Ay-Yâfroṭâ Allâyyâ Aḥâdom-Minhom. Aâo Ay-Yâtghā. ^{c}Âzzâ Jārok. Wâtâbārâkâs-mok

Chapter Four

Duʿā' For Special Occasions

O Allāh! Lord of the Seven Firmaments and whatever they cover, Lord of the seven earths and whatever they contain, Creator of the devils and whoever they mislead, Be my Protector from the evil of all Your Creatures lest some of them may hasten with insolence against me or transgress the bounds. Honored is he who is in Your protection and blessed be is Your Name.

After a pleasant dream

(129)

اَلْحَمْدُ لِلّٰهِ الَّذِى بِنِعْمَتِهِ تَتِمُّ الصَّالِحَاتُ

Alḥâmdu-lillāhil-lâthī Bini^{c}mâthī Tâtimmoṣ-ṣāliḥāt

Grace be to Allāh through Whose blessings good things are accomplished.

After an unpleasant dream

(130)

اَلْحَمْدُ لِلّٰهِ عَلٰى كُلِّ حَالٍ

Alḥâmdu-lillāhi-^{c}âlā Kullî-ḥāl

Grace be to Allāh under all circumstances.

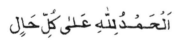

If one wakes up after a nightmare

(131)

أَعُوذُ بِكَلِمَاتِ
اللهِ التَّامَّاتِ مِنْ غَضَبِهِ وَعِقَابِهِ وَشَرِّ عِبَادِهِ ، وَمِنْ
هَمَزَاتِ الشَّيَاطِينِ وَأَنْ يَحْضُرُونِ

A^{c}oothô Bikâlimātil-lāhittāmmāti min Ghâḍâḅihî Wâ^{c}iqābihî-Wâshârrî-^{c}ibādihî Wâmin Hâmâzātish-shâyaṭeen Wâ'an Yâḥḍôroon

I seek refuge in the perfect words of Allāh, from His displeasure and punishment and from evil people, and from the (evil) promptings of devils and from their presence.

II. On Social Occasions

What to say if you see a Muslim brother smiling:

(132)

Aḍḥakallāho Sinnâk — أَضْحَكَ اللهُ سِنَّكَ

May Allāh bring smiles to you.

When one is told "I love you"

(133)

Aḥâbbâkâl-lâthî Aḥbâbtâni Lâh — أَحَبَّكَ الَّذِي أَحْبَبْتَنِي لَهُ

May He, for Whose sake you love me, love you also.

When a favor is done unto us:

(134)

جَزَاكَ اللهُ خَيْرًا

Jâzākâllāho Khâyrân

May Allāh give you a good reward.

What to say to one who got married:

(135)

بَارَكَ اللهُ لَكَ ، وَبَارَكَ عَلَيْكَ ، وَجَمَعَ بَيْنَكُمَا فِي خَيْرٍ

Bārâkâ-llāho-lâk. Wâbārâkâ ^{c}âlâyk. Wâjâmâ^{c}ā Bâynâkômā Fī-khâyr

May Allāh bless (your spouse) for you; and may He bless you and join you in a happy union.

At the beginning of sexual intercourse:

(136)

بِسْمِ اللهِ ، اللَّهُمَّ جَنِّبْنَا الشَّيْطَانَ وَجَنِّبِ الشَّيْطَانَ مَا رَزَقْتَنَا

Bismillāh. Allāhommâ Jânnibnâsh-Shâyṭān. Wâjânnibish-shâyṭānâ-mā Râzâqtânâ

In the name of Allāh. O Allāh! Keep us away from Satan, and keep Satan away from what You bestow on us (our children).

Prayer for small children

(137)

أُعِيذُكَ بِكَلِمَاتِ اللهِ التَّامَّةِ ، مِنْ كُلِّ شَيْطَانٍ وَهَامَّةٍ
وَمِنْ كُلِّ عَيْنٍ لَامَّةٍ

O[c]eethôkâ Bịkâlimātil-lāhit-tāmmâh. Min kullî-shâyṭānin-Wâhāmmâh Wâmin Kulli-[c]âynin Lāmmâh

I seek refuge for you in the perfect words of Allāh, from every devil and every poisonous reptile, and from every bad eye.

At the end of meetings or gatherings

(138)

سُبْحَانَكَ اللّٰهُمَّ وَبِحَمْدِكَ اَشْهَدُ اَنْ لَّا اِلٰهَ
اِلَّا اَنْتَ اَسْتَغْفِرُكَ وَاَتُوْبُ اِلَيْكَ

Suḅḥānâkâl-lāhommâ Wâbiḥâmdik. Ash-hâdo-Allā Ilāha-illa Ant. Astâghfirokâ-Wâ'âtoobo Ilâyk

Glory and praise be to You, O Allāh! I bear witness that there is no deity except You. I beg of You Your forgiveness and I repent to You.

III. On the Occasion of Travel

What to say to one who is leaving

(139)

أَستَوْدِعُ اللهَ دِينَكَ :

وَأَمَانَتَكَ ، وَخَوَاتِيمَ عَمَلِكَ ، وَأَقْرَأُ عَلَيْكَ السَّلَامَ

Astâwdî^c ollâhâ Deenâkâ Wâ'amānâtâkâ Wâkhâwāteemâ ^c amâlik Wâ'âqrâ'o ^c âlâykâs-sālām.

Unto Allāh do I commend your deen (Islam), your trust (i.e. family, property,... etc.), and the conclusions of your deeds, and I recite salām (peace) upon you.

(140)

زَوَّدَكَ اللهُ التَّقْوَى ،

وَغَفَرَ ذَنْبَكَ ، وَيَسَّرَ لَكَ الْخَيْرَ حَيْثُمَا كُنْتَ

Zâwwâdâkâl-lahot-tâqwa Wâghâfârâ-Thânbâk Wâyâssârâ Lâkâl-Khâyrâ Ḥaythomā Kunt

May Allāh provide you with taqwa (Allāh-consciousness), forgive your sins, and facilitate good for you wherever you may be.

When bidding farewell (by the traveller)

(141)

أَستَوْدِعُكَ اللهَ الَّذِى لَا تَضِيعُ وَدَائِعُهُ

Astaodi^c okâllahâ-âllâthī La Tâḍee ^c ô Wâda'i^c ôh

I commend you unto Allāh Whose trusts are never lost.

What to say when setting out on a journey

(142)

اللَّهُمَّ بِكَ أَصُولُ ، وَبِكَ
أَجُولُ ، وَبِكَ أَسِيرُ . اللَّهُمَّ إِنِّي أَسأَلُكَ فِي سَفَرِي
هٰذَا البِرَّ وَالتَّقْوَى ، وَمِنَ الْعَمَلِ مَا تَرْضَى اللَّهُمَّ هَوِّنْ
عَلَيْنَا سفرنَا هٰذَا وَاطْوِ عَنَّا بُعْدَهُ اللَّهُمَّ أَنْتَ الصَّاحِبُ
فِي السَّفَرِ وَالْخَلِيفَةُ فِي الْأَهْلِ . اللَّهُمَّ إِنِّي أَعُوذُ بِكَ
مِنْ وَعْثَاءِ السَّفَرِ ، وَكَآبَةِ الْمَنْظَرِ ، وَسوءِ الْمُنقَلَبِ
فِي الْمَالِ وَالْأَهْلِ وَالْوَلَدِ

Allāhoma Bîka Aṣool. Wâbîkâ Ajool. Wâbîka Aseer. Allāhomâ Innî As'alokâ Fi Sâfârî-Hāthâl-Birrâ-Wâttâqwā. Wâmînâl ^{c}âmâlî Mā Tarḍā. Allāhommâ-Hâwwin ^{c}âlâynā Sâfârânā-Hāthā Wâṭwî-^{c}ânnā Bo^{c}dâh. Allāhommâ-Antâṣ-ṣāhibû-Fis-sâfâr. Wâlkhâleefâtû Fil-Ahl. Allāhommâ-Inni A^{c}oothô Bîkâ Min Wa^{c}thā'is-sâfâr, Wâkâ'ābâtil-mânzar Wâsoo'il-Monqâlâbî Fil-Ahlî Wâlmālî-Wâlwâlâd

O Allāh! It is with Your help that I struggle, move and walk. O Allāh! I beg of You in this journey, virtue, piety, and deeds which are acceptable to You. O Allāh! Make our journey easy for us and shorten for us its distance. O Allāh! You are the Companion in the Journey and the Guardian-Protector of the household. O Allāh! I seek refuge in You from the difficulties of this journey, and from disagreeable sights and from unpleasant return to (my) wealth, household and children.

Upon return from a journey

Repeat the previous du^{c}ā' and add to it:

(143)

ايِبُوْنَ تَائِبُوْنَ عَابِدُوْنَ لِرَبِّنَا حَامِدُوْنَ

Āyiboon, Tā'eboon, ^{c}ābîdoon, lîrâbbinā Ḥāmidoon

We are returners, repentants, worshippers and thankful to our Lord.

IV. In Distress

When faced by a hardship

(144)

اللَّهُمَّ لَا سَهْلَ إِلَّا مَا جَعَلْتَهُ سَهْلاً ، وَأَنْتَ تَجْعَلُ الْحَزْنَ
إِذَا شِئْتَ سَهْلاً

Allāhommâlā-Sâhlâ Illā-mā-Jâ^{c}âltâho Sâhlâ Wâ'ntâ Tâj^{c}âlôl-ḥâznâ Ithā Shi'tâ Sâhlâ

O Allāh! There is nothing easy except what You make easy, and You make the difficult easy if it be Your will.

When one's desire or hope could not be fulfilled

(145)

قَدَّرَ اللهُ وَمَا شَاءَ فَعَلَ

Qâddârâl-lāhô Wâmā Shā'â-fâᶜâl

Allāh had decided, and whatever He willed, He did.

When feeling angry:

(146)

أَعُوذُ بِاللهِ مِنَ الشَّيْطٰنِ الرَّجِيمِ

Âᶜoothô Billāhî-minâsh-shâyṭānir-râjeem

I seek refuge in Allāh from the accursed Satan.

When one is overwhelmed by a problem

(147)

حَسْبُنَا اللهُ وَنِعْمَ الْوَكِيلُ

Ḥâsbonâl-lāho Wâneᶜmâl-wâkeel

Allāh suffices us and He is the best Guardian.

When in pain

(148)

بِسْمِ اللهِ ثَلَاثَ مَرَّاتٍ ، أَعُوذُ بِعِزَّةِ
اللهِ وَقُدْرَتِهِ مِنْ شَرِّ مَا أَجِدُ وَأُحَاذِرُ سَبْعَ مَرَّاتٍ

(While placing one's hand over the location of pain)

Bismillāh (3 times)
A[c]oothô Bî[c]izzatil-lāhi Wâqodrâtihi Min shârrî-mā Ajîdu Wâ'oḥaẓir (7 times)

In the name of Allāh

I seek refuge in exalted power and glory of Allāh from that which I feel and fear.

When visiting a sick person

(149)

اللّهُمَّ أَذْهِبَ الْبَاسَ

رَبَّ النَّاسِ ، اشْفِ وَأَنْتَ الشَّافِي ، لَاشِفَاءَ إِلَّا شِفَاؤُكَ ،

شِفَاءً لَا يُغَادِرُ سِقَماً

Allāhommâ Ath-hibil-bās Râbban-nās. Ishfî Wâ'antâsh-shāfī Lā-Shifā'â-illā-Shifā'ok. Shifā'al-lāyoghādirô-Sâqâmā

O Allāh! Remove the hardship, O Lord of mankind. Grant cure for You are the Healer. There is no cure but from You, cure which leaves no illness behind. (While patting the sick person.)

At the time of a disaster

(150)

إِنَّا لِلّهِ وَإِنَّا إِلَيْهِ رَاجِعُونَ ، اللّهُمَّ عِنْدَكَ أَحْتَسِبُ مُصِيبَتِي

فَأْجُرْنِي فِيهَا وَأَبْدِلْنِي مِنْهَا خَيْرًا

Innā-lillāhî-Wâ'innā Ilâyhî-raji[c]oon. Allāhommâ-[c]indâkâ Aḥtasibû-muṣeebâti. Fâ'jorni Fîhā Wâ'abdilini Minhā-khâyrâ

To Allāh we belong, and to Him is our return. O Allāh! You suffice me in disaster. So reward me for it and replace it with something which is good.

When offering condolence (to the family of the deceased)

(151)

إِنَّ لِلّٰهِ مَا أَخَذَ وَلَهُ مَا أَعْطَى وَكُلُّ شَيْءٍ عِنْدَهُ
بِأَجَلٍ مُسَمًّى فَلْتَصْبِرْ وَلْتَحْتَسِبْ

Innâ-lillāhî-mā-akhâthâ Wâlâho-mā-a^cṭā. Wâkkollo-Shây'in ^cindâho Bi'ajâlim-musâmmā- Fâltaṣbir Wâltaḥtasib

Due is to Allāh that which He has taken away and His is whatever He has given. With Him, everything has an appointed term; so have patience and seek reward from Him.

When visiting the graveyard

(152)

السَّلَامُ عَلَيْكُمْ
أَهْلَ الدِّيَارِ مِنَ الْمُؤْمِنِينَ وَالْمُسْلِمِينَ ، وَيَرْحَمُ اللهُ
الْمُسْتَقْدِمِينَ مِنْكُمْ وَالْمُسْتَأْخِرِينَ ، وَإِنَّا إِنْ شَاءَ اللهُ
بِكُمْ لَاحِقُونَ ، أَسْأَلُ اللهَ لَنَا وَلَكُمُ الْعَافِيَةَ ،
أَنْتُمْ لَنَا فَرَطٌ وَنَحْنُ لَكُمْ تَبَعٌ ، اللَّهُمَّ لَا تَحْرِمْنَا
أَجْرَهُمْ ، وَلَا تُضِلَّنَا بَعْدَهُمْ

Assâlmô-^{c}âlâykum Ahlâd-diyāri-minâl-Mu'mineenâ-Wâlmuslimeen. Wâyârḥâmol-lāhol-mustâqdimeenâ-minkum Wâlmusta'khireen. Wa'innā In shāâllāhô-bîkum Lāḥiqoon. As'alol-lāhâ-lânā Wâlâkumul-^{c}afiyâh. Antom lânā fârâṭon. Wânâḥnô-lâkum-tâba^{c}on. Allāhommâ Lā Taḥrimnā Ajrâhom Wâlā Tuḍillânā Bâ^{c}dâhom

Peace be upon you dwellers of these abodes, believers and Muslims. May Allāh have mercy on those of you who were first (to die) and those who were last. We will, whenever Allāh wills, join you. I beg of Allāh salvation for us and for you. You preceded us and we will follow you. O Allāh! Deprive us not from reward (similar to theirs) and lead us not astray after they are gone.

V. Others

Prayer for fulfilment of a need (Ṣalātul-Ḥajāh)

(153)

مَنْ كَانَتْ لَهُ حَاجَةٌ إِلَى اللهِ تَعَالَى أَوْ إِلَى أَحَدٍ مِنْ
بَنِي آدَمَ ، فَلْيَتَوَضَّأْ وَلْيُحْسِنْ وُضُوءَهُ ، ثُمَّ لِيُصَلِّ
رَكْعَتَيْنِ ، ثُمَّ يُثْنِي عَلَى اللهِ تَعَالَى ، وَلْيُصَلِّ عَلَى النَّبِيِّ
صَلَّى اللهُ عَلَيْهِ وَسَلَّمَ وَلْيَقُلْ : لَا إِلَهَ إِلَّا اللهُ الْحَلِيمُ
الْكَرِيمُ ، سُبْحَانَ اللهِ رَبِّ الْعَرْشِ الْعَظِيمِ ،
الْحَمْدُ لِلَّهِ رَبِّ الْعَالَمِينَ ، أَسْأَلُكَ مُوجِبَاتِ رَحْمَتِكَ[1]
وَعَزَائِمَ مَغْفِرَتِكَ ، وَالْعِصْمَةَ مِنْ كُلِّ ذَنْبٍ ،

وَالْغَنِيمَةَ مِنْ كُلِّ بِرٍّ ، وَالسَّلَامَةَ مِنْ كُلِّ إِثْمٍ ،
لَا تَدَعْ لِي ذَنْبًا إِلَّا غَفَرْتَهُ ، وَلَا هَمًّا إِلَّا فَرَّجْتَهُ ، وَلَا حَاجَةً
هِيَ لَكَ رِضًا إِلَّا قَضَيْتَهَا يَا أَرْحَمَ الرَّاحِمِينَ ،
ثُمَّ يَسْأَلُ مِنْ أَمْرِ الدُّنْيَا وَالْآخِرَةِ مَا شَاءَ فَإِنَّهُ يُقَدَّرُ

Alḥâmdulillāhî Râbbil-^{c}ālâmeen. Allāhomâ sâllî ^{c}alā Muhâmmâd (S.A.W.). Lā Ilāha-illâl-lāhul ḥâleemul-kâreem. Subḥānâllāh – î Râbbil-^{c}arshil-^{c}âzeem. Alḥâmdulillāhi-râbbil-^{c}ālâmeen. As'âlokâ Mūjibātî-râḥmâtik. Wâ^{c}âzā'imâ Maghfirâtik. Wâl^{c}iṣmâtâ min kullî-thâmb. Wâlghâneemâtâ min kullî-birr. Wâssâlāmâtâ min Kulli-ithm. Lā Tâdâ^{c}-il thâmbân illā Ghâfârtâh. Wâlā Hâmmân Illā Fârrâjtâh. Wâlā hājâtân Heya Lâkâ-riḍan Illa Qaḍâytâhā Yā Arḥâmârrāḥimeen.

Praise be to Allāh, Lord of the Universe. May Allāh's peace and blessing be upon Muhm̂mâd (S.A.W.). There is no deity but Allāh, Most-Forebearing, Supreme in Honour. Glory be to Allāh, Lord of the Great Throne. Praise be to Allāh, Lord of the Universe. O Allāh! I seek of You the means of (deserving) Your mercy, the means of (ascertaining) Your forgiveness, the protection from all mistakes, the benefit from all virtue and the freedom from all sins. O Allāh! Leave no mistake of mine without Your forgiveness, nor any stress without Your relief, nor any need of which You approve without being fulfilled by You, O Most Merciful of the merciful.

[After reciting this du^{c}ā', one should state the specific need for which the du^{c}ā' was made]

When seeking guidance in decision-making (Isti-khārâh)

(154)

« اللَّهُمَّ إِنِّي أَسْتَخِيرُكَ بِعِلْمِكَ ، وَأَسْتَقْدِرُكَ بِقُدْرَتِكَ ،
وَأَسْأَلُكَ مِنْ فَضْلِكَ الْعَظِيمِ ، فَإِنَّكَ تَقْدِرُ وَلَا
أَقْدِرُ ، وَتَعْلَمُ وَلَا أَعْلَمُ ، وَأَنْتَ عَلَّامُ الْغُيُوبِ .
اللَّهُمَّ إِنْ كُنْتَ تَعْلَمُ أَنَّ هَذَا الْأَمْرَ خَيْرٌ لِي فِي دِينِي
وَمَعَاشِي وَعَاقِبَةِ أَمْرِي - أَوْ قَالَ عَاجِلِ أَمْرِي
وَآجِلِهِ - فَاقْدُرْهُ لِي وَيَسِّرْهُ لِي ثُمَّ بَارِكْ لِي فِيهِ ؛ وَإِنْ
كُنْتَ تَعْلَمُ أَنَّ هَذَا الْأَمْرَ شَرٌّ لِي فِي دِينِي وَمَعَاشِي
وَعَاقِبَةِ أَمْرِي - أَوْ قَالَ فِي عَاجِلِ أَمْرِي وَآجِلِهِ -
فَاصْرِفْهُ عَنِّي ، وَاصْرِفْنِي عَنْهُ ، وَاقْدُرْ لِيَ الْخَيْرَ
حَيْثُ كَانَ ثُمَّ أَرْضِنِي بِهِ » .

Allāhommâ Innî Astâkheerokâ Bi[c]ilmik. Wa'astâq-dirokâ Bîqodrâtik. Wa'as'alokâ Min Faḍlikâl-[c]âzeem. Fa'innâka Tâqdirû Wâlā Aqdîr. Wâtâ[c]lâmo Wâlā-â[c]lâm. Wa'antâ-[c]allāmul ghuyoob.

Allāhommâ In Kûntâ Tâ[c]lamû Annâ [Hāthâl-Amrâ] Khayul-lee Fî Deenee Wâmâ[c]ashî Wâ[c]ajilâ Amrî Wa'ājilâh, Fâqdorhô lee, Wayâssirhô lee, Thommâ-bārik lee fih.

Wa'in Kontâ Ta^c^lâmô Annâ [Hāthâl-Amrâ] sẖârrul-lee Fî Deẹnee. Wâmâ^c^āshī. Wa^c^ājilâ Amrī. Wa'ājilahô. Faṣrifhô ^c^ânnee. Wâsrifnee ^c^ânh. Wâqdûr lêyâl-khâyr Haytḣô kān. Tḣômmâ ardînī Bîh.

O Allāh! I seek Your guidance (in making a choice) by virtue of Your knowledge, and I seek ability by virtue of Your power, and I ask You of Your great bounty. You have power, I have none. And You know, I know not. You are the Knower of hidden things.

O Allāh! If in Your knowledge, (this matter) is good for my religion, my livelihood and my affairs; immediate and in the distant, then ordain for me, make it easy for me and bless it for me. And if in Your knowledge, (this matter) is bad for my religion, my livelihood and my affairs; immediate and in the distant, then turn it away from me, and turn me away from it. And ordain for me the good wherever it be and make me pleased with it.

Notes:

1. The above du^c^ā' is to be recited when there is uncertainty about the advisability of taking a decision, provided it is Islamically permissible.

2. After performing wuḍū' (ablution), one should offer two râk^c^âhs (sunnâh required for this purpose).

3. Before reciting the du^c^ā' it should be made sure that the person is not already inclined to a given decision; otherwise it will mean that the person is not serious about seeking guidance of Allāh (S.W.T.).

4. In making this du^c^ā' the actual matter or decision concerning which divine guidance is being sought should be mentioned instead of the words (Hāthâl Amrâ) in transliteration or the words "this matter" in the translation above.

5. After reciting the du^c^ā' (immediately or later on), one may feel more favorably disposed towards one choice or the other.

When one wakes up for night prayers (Tâhâjjud)

(155)

اللَّهُمَّ لَكَ الْحَمْدُ أَنْتَ قَيِّمُ السَّمٰوَاتِ
وَالْأَرْضِ وَمَنْ فِيهِنَّ ، وَلَكَ الْحَمْدُ لَكَ مُلْكُ السَّمٰوَاتِ
وَالْأَرْضِ وَمَنْ فِيهِنَّ ، وَلَكَ الْحَمْدُ أَنْتَ نُورُ السَّمٰوَاتِ
وَالْأَرْضِ وَمَنْ فِيهِنَّ ، وَلَكَ الْحَمْدُ أَنْتَ الْحَقُّ ، وَوَعْدُكَ
الْحَقُّ ، وَلِقَاؤُكَ حَقٌّ ، وَقَوْلُكَ حَقٌّ ، وَالْجَنَّةُ حَقٌّ وَالنَّارُ
حَقٌّ ، وَالنَّبِيُّونَ حَقٌّ ، وَمُحَمَّدٌ صلى الله عليه وسلم حَقٌّ ،
وَالسَّاعَةُ حَقٌّ ، اللَّهُمَّ لَكَ أَسْلَمْتُ ، وَبِكَ آمَنْتُ ، وَعَلَيْكَ
تَوَكَّلْتُ ، وَإِلَيْكَ أَنَبْتُ ، وَبِكَ خَاصَمْتُ ، وَإِلَيْكَ
حَاكَمْتُ ، فَاغْفِرْ لِي مَا قَدَّمْتُ وَمَا أَخَّرْتُ ، وَمَا أَسْرَرْتُ
وَمَا أَعْلَنْتُ ، وَمَا أَنْتَ أَعْلَمُ بِهِ مِنِّي ، أَنْتَ الْمُقَدِّمُ
وَأَنْتَ الْمُؤَخِّرُ ، لَا إِلٰهَ إِلَّا أَنْتَ ، وَلَا حَوْلَ وَلَا قُوَّةَ
إِلَّا بِاللَّهِ

Allāhommâ lâkâl-Hâmd. Antâ Qâyyimâs-sâmāwātî wâl'arḍi- Wâmā Fīhinn. Wâkâkâl-Ḥm̂dû Lâkâ Mulkus-sâmāwāti Wâl'arḍî-Wâmân Fīhinn. Wâlâkâl-Ḥâmd. Antâ noorôssâmāwātî-wal'ardi-Wâmân Fīhinn. Wâlâkâl-Ḥâmdû antâl-ḥâqq. Wâwâ[c]dokâl ḥâqq. Wâliqā'okâ hâqq. Wâqaolokâ-ḥâqq. Wâljânnâtu-ḥâqq. Wânnāru-ḥâqq. Wânnâbiyyoonâ-hâqq. Wâmuḥâmmâdun Sâllâl-lāho [c]alâyhî wâsâllâmâ hâqq Wâssā[c]âtô-ḥâqq.

Allāhomâ-lâkâ Aslâmt. Wâbîkâ Āmânt. Wâ^{c}âlâykâ-Tâwâkkâlt. Wa'ilâykâ-Anâbt. Wâbîkâ-Khaṣâmt. Wa'ilâykâ-Ḥākâmt. Fâghfir-li Mā-Qâddâmto-wâmā akh-khârt. Wâmā-Asrârto Wâmâ-a^{c}lânt. Wâmā-Antâ-A^{c}lâmo Bihi Minnî. Antâl-Moqâddimu-Wa'antâl-mu'âkh-khir. La-ilāhâ-illā-ânt. Wâlā Ḥâolâ Wâlā Qowwâtâ Illā Billāh.

All Praise is due to You, O Allāh! You are the Sustainer of the heavens and the earth and whatever is in them. Praise be to you; Yours is the domain of the heavens and the earth and whatever is in them. Praise be to You; You are the light of the heavens and the earth and whatever is in them. Praise be to You.

You are the Truth. Your promise is true, meeting with You is true, Your word is true, Paradise is true, hell is true, Prophets are true, Muhâmmâd (S.A.W.) is true, the Hour (of Judgement) is true.

O Allāh! Unto You do I submit, in You do I believe, upon You do I depend, Unto You do I turn. For You do I contend; Unto You do I seek judgement. So forgive me for what I did and will do, for what I concealed and what I declared, and for that of which You are more knowledgeable than me.

You are the expediter and You are the deferrer. There is no deity but You. And there is no ability or power except by the leave of Allāh.

Footnotes

1. Al-Qur'ān, 39:11-12, Directed to Prophet Muhâmmâd (S.A.W.)

2. Al-Qur'ān, 3:53, Prayers of the disciples of Prophet Īsā (Jesus), ^{c}Âlâyhis-Sâlām, in response to his call for helpers.

3. Al-Qur'ān, 18:14, Prayer of the "People of the Cave" in rejection to the polytheism practised by their people.

4. Al-Qur'ān, 5:114, Prayer of the disciples of Prophet ^{c}Īsā, ^{c}Âlâyhis-Sâlām. It shows that all those who bowed to Allāh's will were "Muslims".

5. Al-Qur'ān, , 2:139, In response to Jews and Christians who argued that by becoming Jew or Christian, one is guided to salvation. The preceding Āyāt show that Ibrāhīm (^{c}Âlâyhis-Sâlām), and his descendents were nothing but upright Muslims.

6. Al-Qur'ān, 12:108, Follows Āyāt which point out to those who pass by countless signs of Allāh's presence and attributes. Also to those whose nominal faith in Allāh does not shield them from associating other gods with Allāh (S.W.T.) and deifying mortals.

7. Al-Qur'ān, 43:82, Directed to Prophet Muhâmmâd (S.A.W.). It glorifies Allāh (S.W.T.) from attributing a son to Him.

8. Al-Qur'ān, 59:23, This is part of 3 Āyāt containing 14 of the attributes of Allāh (59:22-24)

9. Al-Qur'ān, 55:78, Concludes Surât-ur-Râḥmān whose basic theme is the Bounty and Majesty of Allāh (S.W.T.) and man's duty to acknowledge them.

10. Al-Qur'ān, 6:100-101, in response to those who made the Jinn equals with Allāh (S.W.T.) and attributed to Him sons and daughters.

11. Al-Qur'ān, 4:171, in rejection of the "trinity".

12. Al-Qur'ān, 23:14, concludes 3 Āyāt which give an amazing description of the fetal stages. For a scientific commentary on these Āyāt (23:12-14) see Maurice Bucaille, *The Bible, The Qur'an and Science.*

13. Al-Qur'ān, 43:85.

14. Al-Qur'an, 25:61.

15. Al-Qur'ān, 7:54. Shows that the establishment of an Islamic government is an acknowledgement of Allāh's right to govern being the Creator.

16. Al-Qur'an, 56:96.

17. Al-Qur'ān, 15:98, Instructions to Prophet Muhâmmâd (S.A.W.) when he was distressed at what the unbelievers said.

18. Al-Qur'an, 17:108, Describes the reaction of the sincere among those who received previous revelations upon hearing the Qur'ān. They saw in the Qur'ān and in Muhâmmâd (S.A.W.) the fulfilment of Allāh's promise in previous scriptures. A booklet on Muhâmmâd in the Bible is forthcoming, Inshā' Allāh.

19. Al-Qur'an, 30:17.

20. Al-Qur'an, 3:191, Believers; reaction when they contemplate the wonders of creation in the heavens and the earth.

21. Al-Qur'an, 36:83, conclusion of Surât Yāsīn. As everything was

created and maintained by Allāh (S.W.T.), so will everything go back to Him.

22. Al-Qur'an, 67:1.

23. Al-Qur'an, 40:64.

24. Al-Qur'an, 87:1.

25. Al-Qur'ān, 110:3, At the glorious moment of the Prophet's return to Mâkkâh, and when people were embracing Islām in crowds, the Prophet (S.A.W.) is reminded to humbly praise Allāh for the victory He gave to the believers.

26. Al-Qur'an, 64:1.

27. Al-Qur'an, 11:123.

28. Al-Qur'an, 11:56, Prayer of Prophet Hood, ᶜÂlâyhis-Sâlām.

29. Al-Qur'an, 67:29.

30. Al-Qur'an, 3:20.

31. Al-Qur'an, 7:191.

32. Al-Qur'an, 6:79, Prayer of Prophet Ibrāhīm, ᶜÂlâyhis-Sâlām.

33. Al-Qur'ān, 6:162-163.

34. Al-Qur'ān, 14:38, Prayer of Prophet Ibrāhīm, Alâysis-Sâlām.

35. Al-Qur'an, 39:46.

36. Al-Qur'ān, 26:78-82.

37. Al-Qur'ān, 25:58.

38. Al-Qur'ān, 6:77, Prayer of Prophet Ibrāhîm, Alâyhis-Sâlām, in his search for truth and certitude.

39. Al-Qur'ān, 28:22, Prayer of Prophet Musā, ^{c}Âlâyhis-Sâlām, when he left Egypt in a state of fear, turning towards the land of Mâdyân.

40. Al-Qur'ān, 18:10, Prayer of the "People of the Cave" when they went to the Cave.

41. Al-Qur'ān, 3:8, It comes after warning in the previous Āyâh of those "in whose hearts is perversity" who follow the allegorical portions of the Qur'ān, "seeking discord and searching for its hidden meanings" which are known only to Allāh (S.W.T.). It should be noted that in the above Āyah (3:7) there is a mandatory pause (waqf lāzîm) after the word "Allāh". This means that the hidden meanings of the allegorical portions of the Qur'ān are known exclusively to Allāh (S.W.T.) and not shared even by the "those who are firmly grounded in knowledge."

42. Al-Qur'ān, 21:87, This was the cry of Prophet Yūnus (Jonah), ^{c}Âlâyhis-Sâlām, when he was swallowed by a big fish (or whale).

43. Al-Qur'ān, 28:16

44. Al-Qur'ān, 3:16.

45. Al-Qur'ān, 68:29, This was the cry of the rich "People of the Garden" who resolved to gather the fruits of the garden early in the morning before any indigent person come to request a share of the fruits. Overnight, Allāh destroyed their garden. Next morning they were shocked to see their garden like a desolate spot, at which time they realized the cause of their loss, greed.

46. Al-Qur'an, 2:286, This Āyâh along with 2; 284, 285 are highly recommended for recitation at the beginning of the day and in the evening. (At-Tabârani, Al-Hakim).

47. Al-Qur'an, 59:10.

48. Al-Qur'an, 23:118.

49. Al-Qur'an, 7:143, Prayer of Prophet Mūsa, Alâyhis-Sâlām, upon recovering from a swoon in which he fell after asking Allāh (S.W.T.) to let (Musa) look at Him.

50. Al-Qur'an, 2:285.

51. Al-Qur'an, 20:114.

52. Al-Qur'an, 26:83, Prayer of Prophet Ibrahim, [c]Âlâyhis-Sâlām.

53. Al-Qur'an, 44:12, Reference to people's cry during a (prophesised) famine which actually befell the Makkans. May also refer to the day of resurrection.

54. Al-Qur'an, 12:86, Response of Prophet Ya[c]qoob (Jacob), [c]Âlâyhis-Sâlam, when he was criticized by his children for endangering health by continuing to remember his absent son, Yusuf (Joseph).

55. Al-Qur'ān, 2:250, The Prayer of the remaining Israelites who stayed with their commander, Ṭalut (Saul) when they advanced to meet Jalūt (Goliath) and his forces.

56. Al-Qur'ān, 7:206, Prayer of the Egyptian sorcerers (magicians) who believed in Prophet Musa, [c]Âlâyhis-Sâlam, when their pharoah threatened them of mutilation and crucifiction.

57. Al-Qur'ān, 16:137-138.

58. Al-Qur'ān, 17:96.

59. Al-Qur'ān, Prayer of the apostles in the face of their peoples' rejection of the truth.

60. Al-Qur'ān, 28:24, Prayer of Prophet Mūsa, ^{c}Âlâyhis-Sâlām, when he reached Mâdyân tired, homeless, hungry, and in desperate need of help.

61. Al-Qur'ān, 20:25-28, Prayer of Prophet Mūsa, ^{c}Âlâyhis-Sâlām when he received Allāh's command in Sinai to go to the Pharoah and point out his transgression.

62. Al-Qur'ān, 34:41, The response of the angels in the Day of Judgement when Allāh (S.W.T.) asked them "was it you that these men used to worship?"

63. Al-Qur'ān, 9:129, Recitation of this du^{c}ā' seven times in the morning and seven times in the evening is recommended by the Prophet (S.A.W.) as a means of seeking the protection of Allāh from anything which worries us.

64. Al-Qur'ān, 11:47, Prayer of Prophet Nooḥ (Noah), ^{c}Âlâyhis-Sâlām, when he was grieving for the drowning of his unbelieving son.

65. Al-Qur'ān, 12:64, Prayer of Prophet Ya^{c}qoob (Jacob), ^{c}Âlâyhis-Sâlām when his children asked him to send their younger brother (Benjamin) with them to Egypt to get more grain.

66. Al-Qur'ān, 23:97-98.

67. Al-Qur'an, 12:101, Prayer of Prophet Yūsef (Joseph), ^{c}Âlâyhis-Sâlām after reuniting with his family.

68. Al-Qur'ān, 25:65, Prayer of the righteous.

69. Al-Qur'ān, 10:85-86, Prayer of Mūsa's followers in the face of Pharoah's persecution.

70. & 71. Recitation of these two Surahs along with Surat-ul-Ikhlāṣ (§112), 3 times each, is highly recommended in the morning and evening (for protection). Abu-Dāwood, At-Tirmithī, An-Nasā'ī.

72. Al-Qur'ān, 39:66.

73. Al-Qur'ān, 27:40, Prayer of Prophet Sulâyman (Solomon), cÂlâyhis-Sâlām, when he saw the throne of Balqis (the queen of Sheba) before him.

74. Al-Qur'ān, 45:36-37.

75. Al-Qur'ān, 7:43 A prayer of believers in Paradise who believed and worked righteousness.

76. Al-Qur'ān, 28:70.

77. Al-Qur'ān, 21:89, Prayer of Prophet Zâkâriyyā, cÂlâyhis-Sâlām, expressing his desire to have a son. He was blessed with Yâḥyā (John the Baptist).

78. Al-Qur'ān, 37:100, Prayer of Prophet Ibrāhim, cÂlâyhis-Sâlām.

79. Al-Qur'ān, 3:38, Prayer of Prophet Zakariyya, cÂlâyhis-Sâlām.

80. Al-Qur'ān, 25:74

81. Al-Qur'ān, 2:128.

82. Al-Qur'ān, 14:40-41, Prayer of Prophet Ibrāhim, cÂlâysis-Sâlām.

83. Al-Qur'ān, 46:15, Prayer of the believer upon reaching the age of 40.

84. Al-Qur'ān, 17:24, Prayer for parents.

85. Al-Qur'ān, 71:28, Prayer of Prophet Nooh (Noah), cÂlâyhis-Sâlām.

86. Al-Qur'ān, 2:201.

87. Al-Qur'ān, 7:156, Prayer of Prophet Mūsa, cÂlâyhis-Sâlām after rebuking the Israelites for their backsliding to idolatory.

88. Al-Qur'ān, 7:89 Response of the people of Prophet Shucâyb when they were threatened by their countrymen.

89. Al-Qur'ān, 40:7-9, Prayer of the angels on behalf of the believers.

90. Ibn-us-Sunni, Al-Bâzzār. In the evening the word Aṣbaḥnā is changed to Amsâynā (we begin the evening), and the word aṣbâḥâ is changed to Amsā.

91. Abdullah (son of Imām Ahmad). In the evening the word Aṣbaḥnā is changed to Amsâyna.

92. Ibn-us-Sunni. In the evening the word Aṣbâḥto is changed to Amsâyto.

93. Abu-Dāwood, An-Nasā'ī, Ibn-Ḥibbān. In the evening the word Aṣbâḥâ is changed to Amsā.

94. Aḥmâd, Ibn-Mājah.

95. Abu-Dāwood, At-Tirmithī, An-Nasā'ī, Al-Ḥākim.

96. Muslim. Highly rewarded du^{c}ā'.

97. Abu-Dawood, At-Tirmithī. Excellent du^{c}ā' for seeking the protection of Allāh.

98. Aḥmad, Aṭ-Ṭâbarāni.

99. Ibn Ḥibbān.

100. Abu-Dāwood. Excellent du^{c}ā' for one who is worried or in debt.

101. & 102. Abu-Dawood.

103. Al-Bukhāri. The Prophet (S.A.W.) called "the Master du^{c}ā' for seeking forgiveness".

104. Abu-Dāwood, At-Tirmithī, Al-Hākim.

105. Aṭ-Ṭabarāni.

106. At-Tirmithī.

107. Aḥmâd, Aṭ-Ṭâbârāni. This du^{c}ā' is recommended after Fâjr and Mâghrib prayers.

108. An-Nasā'ī, Aṭ-Ṭabarāni, Al-Hākim. This du^{c}ā' is recommended at the end of meetings. It atones for one's infractions during the meeting.

109. Al-Bukhāri.

110. Al-Bukhari, Muslim.

111. Abu-Dāwood.

112. An-Nasā'ī.

113. Muslim, At-Tirmithī.

114. Al-Bukhāri.

115. Abu-Dāwood, At-Tirmithī, An-Nasa'ī.

116. Al-Bukhāri.

117. Muslim, Abu-Dāwood, An-Nasā'i.

118. Muslim.

119. Muslim, Abu-Dāwood, An-Nasā'ī.

120. Abu-Dāwood.

121. Ibn-us-Sunni.

122. Abu-Dāwood, At-Tirmithī, An-Nasā'i, Ibn-Mājâh.

123. Ibn-us-Sunni.

124. Ibn-us-Sunni.

125. Al-Qur'ān, 43:13.

126. Al-Bukhāri, Muslim, Abu-Dāwood, At-Tirmithī, An-Nasā'i, Ibn Mājâh.

127. Ibn-Hibbān, Aṭ-Tâbârāni.

128. Aṭ-Ṭâbārāni.

129. Al-Ḥakim, Ibn-Mājâh.

130. Al-Hākim, Ibn-Mājâh.

131. Abu-Dāwood, At-Tirmithī, An-Nasā'i.

132. Al-Bukhāri, Muslim.

133. Abu-Dāwood, An-Nâsā'i, Ibn-Ḥibbān.

134. At-Tirmithī.

135. Al-Bukhāri, Muslim.

136. Al-Bukhāri.

137. Al-Bukhāri.

138. Abu-Dāwood, Al-Hākim.

139. At-Tirmithī, An-Nasā'i (narrated by ^{c}Abdullah b. ^{c}ômâr).

140. At-Tirmithī, An-Nasā'ī (narrated by Anas).

141. Aṭ-Ṭâbarāni (narrated by Abi-Hurâyrâh).

142. Ahmâd, Muslim (narrated by ^{c}Ali, Ibn ^{c}Omar and others).

143. Ibid.

144. Ibn-Ḥibbān.

145. An-Nâsā'i.

146. Al-Bukhāri, Muslim.

147. Abu-Dāwood.

148. Muslim.

149. Al-Bukhāri.

150. At-Tirmithī, Al-Hākim.

151. Al-Bukhāri.

152. Muslim, An-Nasā'i, Ibn-Mājâh.

153. At-Tirmithī, An-Nasā'ī, Ibn Mājah.

154. Al-Bukhāri.

155. Al-Bukhāri.